17

General John J. Pershing

Field Marshal Sir Douglas Haig

General Franchet D'Esperey

Marshal Ferdinand Foch

General Armando Diaz

General Sir E. H. H. Allenby

General H. J. M. Marshall

THE VICTORIOUS GENERALS

General Foch, Commander-in-Chief of all Allied forces. General Pershing, Commander-in-Chief of the American armies. Field Marshal Haig, head of the British armies. General d'Esperey (French) to whom Bulgaria surrendered. General Diaz, Commander-in-Chief of the Italian armies. General Marshall (British), head of the Mesopotamian expedition. General Allenby (British), who redeemed Palestine from the Turks.

HISTORY OF THE WORLD WAR

An Authentic Narrative of
The World's Greatest War

By FRANCIS A. MARCH, Ph.D.

In Collaboration with

RICHARD J. BEAMISH

Special War Correspondent
and Military Analyst

With an Introduction

By GENERAL PEYTON C. MARCH
Chief of Staff of the United States Army

Illustrated with Reproductions from
the Official Photographs of the United
States, British and French Governments

THE SMITHSONIAN COMPANY
OAKLAND, CAL.

AMERICA'S PARTICIPATION IN THE WORLD WAR

In illustrating the book due consideration has been given to important personages, scenes and incidents of the World War, in which Americans participated.   In looking at these pictures, one feels the same thrill of delight that the French people must have felt at the scenes depicted in the photograph entitled, "The Arrival of a United States Transport, the Largest Ship in the World, Carrying 12,000 American Soldiers."   The illustrations of Chateau-Thierry, St. Mihiel and other scenes of heroic activity in which Americans were engaged, will be viewed with pride by every American; for there is hardly a family in the land, who has not been represented by someone in whom they have a deep interest, and who was associated in some way with the varied activities of the war.

Note the portraits of Leading American Generals.   General Peyton C. March, the center figure, is the brother of Francis A. March, the author of this book.   He is the highest officer in the United States Army, and one of three who have the right to wear four stars on their shoulder-straps; the only others being Generals Pershing and Bliss.   Their only predecessors in this rank were Generals Washington, Grant, Sherman and Sheridan. The distinguished authorship of this book is a guarantee of its authenticity. The greatest care has been exercised to secure illustrations, portraits, and maps from official sources, which would tell to the eye the same story which the printed words convey to the mind.

THE ACTIVITIES OF ALL NATIONS AND ON EVERY FRONT

The activities on the many different fronts upon which the war was fought and the operations of the different nations engaged in the war and fully illustrated.   Many of these illustrations are reproductions from the official photographs taken by the American, British, Canadian, French and Italian governments.   The "HISTORY OF THE WORLD WAR" gives the complete story of the magnificent parts played by America, Canada, and by each of the Allies, in the world's greatest and most terrible drama.

NOTE. The complete book contains many additional illustrations, portraits, and maps, which will not be found in this prospectus. The illustrations in the prospectus have been selected as representing the different phases of the war and will, therefore, give some idea of the more than two hundred illustrations, portraits, maps, etc., that will be found in the complete book. The illustrations in themselves, form a Pictorial History of the War. The titles of the pictures should be read with care as they greatly aid in understanding the story told by the illustrations.

JERUSALEM DELIVERED.

On December 11, 1917, the Holy City was entered by the British forces. Following the custom of the Crusaders, General Allenby, commander of the British and Allied forces, made his entry, with his staff and Allied officers, through the Jaffa Gate, on foot.

ANCIENT AND MODERN WARFARE MINGLE IN THE HOLY LAND

The distinctly modern British soldier uses the camel, that extremely ancient beast of burden, to get him over the desert spaces in Palestine. The Imperial Camel Corps gave valuable service in the campaign that led to the capture of Jerusalem.

Photo by International Film Service.

THE SALVATION ARMY ON THE WESTERN FRONT
A shell-proof dugout used as a rest room for soldiers.

© *Press Illustrating Service, N. Y.*

THE Y. M. C. A. IN THE FRONT LINE TRENCHES
Instead of the usual hut the Y. M. C. A. sign beside the trench points the
way to a dugout in which soldiers found the comforts which made the sign of the
triangle famous.

A LETTER FROM HOME

In thousands of France's little stone houses this scene has been duplicated. In the towns and villages soldiers were assigned or "billeted" to the houses of the inhabitants with the result that a deep mutual respect grew up between the two nationalities.

THE STRUGGLE FOR ARMENTIERES

Allied forces holding up a German attack on the Lys Canal. Airplanes flying low peppered the Germans with machine guns and broke up their concentrations, aiding greatly in the severe repulse of the attacking Huns.

AFTER A DRIVE ON THE SOMME

British advancing over the captured German trenches, after heavy artillery fire had reduced them to tangled ruins and crushed their powers of resistance.

From the Introduction:

WAR DEPARTMENT,
OFFICE OF THE CHIEF OF STAFF,
WASHINGTON.

NOVEMBER 14, 1918.

With the signing of the Armistice on November 11, 1918, the World War has been practically brought to an end. The events of the past four years have been of such magnitude that the various steps, the numberless battles, and the growth of Allied power which led up to the final victory are not clearly defined even in the minds of many military men. A history of this great period which will state in an orderly fashion this series of events will be of the greatest value to the future students of the war, and to everyone of the present day who desires to refer in exact terms to matters which led up to the final conclusion.

The war will be discussed and re-discussed from every angle and the sooner such a compilation of facts is available, the more valuable it will be. I understand that this History of the World War intends to put at the disposal of all who are interested, such a compendium of facts of the past period of over four years; and that the system employed in safe-guarding the accuracy of statements contained in it will produce a document of great historical value without entering upon any speculative conclusions as to cause and effect of the various phases of the war or attempting to project into an historical document individual opinions. With these ends in view, this History will be of the greatest value.

P. 6 March.

General,
Chief of Staff,
United States Army.

The pages of this prospectus are subject
to revision and correction in the
complete work.

CONTENTS.

3

CONTENTS

CONTENTS

CONTENTS

CONTENTS

CONTENTS

CONTENTS

FOREWORD

THIS is a popular narrative history of the world's greatest war. Written frankly from the viewpoint of America, it visualizes the bloodiest and most destructive conflict of all the ages from its remote causes to its glorious conclusion and beneficent results. The world-shaking rise of new democracies is set forth, and the enormous national and individual sacrifices producing that resurrection of human equality are detailed.

Two ideals have been before us in the preparation of this necessary work. These are simplicity and thoroughness. It is of no avail to describe the greatest of human events if the description is so confused that the reader loses interest. Thoroughness is an historical essential beyond price. So it is that official documents prepared in many instances upon the field of battle, and others taken from the files of the governments at war, are the basis of this work. Maps and photographs of unusual clearness and high authenticity illuminate the text. All that has gone into war making, into the regeneration of the world, are herein set forth with historical particularity. The stark horrors of Belgium, the blighting terrors of chemical warfare, the governmental restrictions placed upon hundreds of millions of civilians, the war sacrifices falling upon all the civilized peoples of earth, are in these pages.

It is a book that mankind can well read and treasure.

TERRITORY OCCUPIED BY THE ALLIES UNDER THE ARMISTICE OF NOVEMBER 11, 1918

Dotted area, invaded territory of Belgium, France, Luxembourg and Alsace-Lorraine to be evacuated in fourteen days; area in small squares, part of Germany west of the Rhine to be evacuated in twenty-five days and occupied by Allied and U. S. troops; lightly shaded area to east of Rhine, neutral zone; black semi-circles, bridge-heads of thirty kilometers radius in the neutral zone to be occupied by Allied armies.

CHAPTER I

A War for International Freedom

M Y FELLOW COUNTRYMEN: The armistice was signed this morning. Everything for which America fought has been accomplished. The war thus comes to an end."

Speaking to the Congress and the people of the United States, President Wilson made this declaration on November 11, 1918. A few hours before he made this statement, Germany, the empire of blood and iron, had agreed to an armistice, terms of which were the hardest and most humiliating ever imposed upon a nation of the first class. It was the end of a war for which Germany had prepared for generations, a war bred of a philosophy that Might can take its toll of earth's possessions, of human lives and liberties, when and where it will. That philosophy involved the cession to imperial Germany of the best years of young German manhood, the training of German youths to be killers of men. It involved the creation of a military caste, arrogant beyond all precedent, a caste that set its strength and pride against the righteousness of democracy, against the possession of wealth and bodily comforts, a caste that visualized itself as part of a power-mad Kaiser's assumption that he and God were to shape the destinies of earth.

When Marshal Foch, the foremost strategist in the world, representing the governments of the Allies and the United States, delivered to the emissaries of Germany terms upon which they might surrender, he brought to an end the bloodiest, the most destructive and the most beneficent war the world has known. It is worthy of note in this connection that the three great wars in which the United States of America engaged have been wars for freedom. The Revolutionary War was for the liberty of the colonies; the Civil War was waged for the freedom of manhood and for the principle of the indissolubility of the Union; the World War, beginning 1914, was fought for the right of small nations to

13

self-government and for the right of every country to the free use of the high seas.

More than four million American men were under arms when the conflict ended. Of these, more than two million were upon the fields of France and Italy. These were thoroughly trained in the military art. They had proved their right to be considered among the most formidable soldiers the world has known. Against the brown rock of that host in khaki, the flower of German savagery and courage had broken at Château-Thierry. There the high tide of Prussian militarism, after what had seemed to be an irresistible dash for the destruction of France, spent itself in the bloody froth and spume of bitter defeat. There the Prussian Guard encountered the Marines, the Iron Division and the other heroic organizations of America's new army. There German soldiers who had been hardened and trained under German conscription before the war, and who had learned new arts in their bloody trade, through their service in the World War, met their masters in young Americans taken from the shop, the field, and the forge, youths who had been sent into battle with a scant six months' intensive training in the art of war. Not only did these American soldiers hold the German onslaught where it was but, in a sudden, fierce, resistless counter-thrust they drove back in defeat and confusion the Prussian Guard, the Pommeranian Reserves, and smashed the morale of that German division beyond hope of resurrection.

The news of that exploit sped from the Alps to the North Sea Coast, through all the camps of the Allies, with incredible rapidity. "The Americans have held the Germans. They can fight," ran the message. New life came into the war-weary ranks of heroic poilus and into the steel-hard armies of Great Britain. "The Americans are as good as the best. There are millions of them, and millions more are coming," was heard on every side. The transfusion of American blood came as magic tonic, and from that glorious day there was never a doubt as to the speedy defeat of Germany. From that day the German retreat dated. The armistice signed on November 11, 1918, was merely the period finishing the death sentence of German militarism, the first word of which was uttered at Château-Thierry.

Germany's defiance to the world, her determination to

CHAPTER II

The World Suddenly Turned Upside Down

DEMORALIZATION, like the black plague of the middle ages, spread in every direction immediately following the first overt acts of war. Men who were millionaires at nightfall awoke the next morning to find themselves bankrupt through depreciation of their stock-holdings. Prosperous firms of importers were put out of business. International commerce was dislocated to an extent unprecedented in history.

The greatest of hardships immediately following the war, however, were visited upon those who unhappily were caught on their vacations or on their business trips within the area affected by the war. Not only men, but women and children, were subjected to privations of the severest character. Notes which had been negotiable, paper money of every description, and even silver currency suddenly became of little value. Americans living in hotels and pensions facing this sudden shrinkage in their money, were compelled to leave the roofs that had sheltered them. That which was true of Americans was true of all other nationalities, so that every embassy and the office of every consul became a miniature Babel of excited, distressed humanity.

The sudden seizure of railroads for war purposes in Germany, France, Austria and Russia, cut off thousands of travelers in villages that were almost inaccessible. Europeans being comparatively close to their homes, were not in straits as severe as the Americans whose only hope for aid lay in the speedy arrival of American gold. Prices of food soared beyond all precedent and many of these hapless strangers went under. Paris, the brightest and gayest city in Europe, suddenly became the most sombre of dwelling places. No traffic was permitted on the highways at night. No lights were permitted and all the cafés were closed at eight o'clock. The gay capital was placed under iron military rule.

Seaports, and especially the pleasure resorts in France, Belgium and England, were placed under a military supervision. Visitors were ordered to return to their homes and every resort was shrouded with darkness at night. The records of those early days are filled with stories of dramatic happenings.

On the night of July 31st Jean Leon Jaurès, the famous leader of French Socialists, was assassinated while dining in a small restaurant near the Paris Bourse. His assassin was Raoul Villein. Jaurès had been endeavoring to accomplish a union of French and

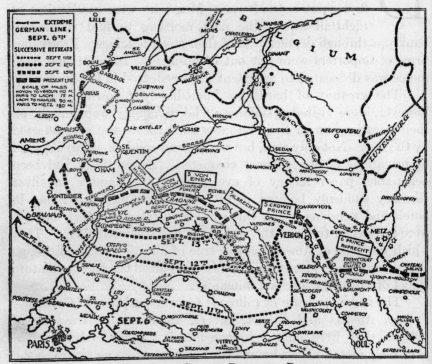

THE FIRST GERMAN DASH FOR PARIS

German Socialists with the aim of preventing the war. The object of the assassination appeared to have been wholly political.

TOURISTS CAUGHT IN THE CATACLYSM

On the same day stock exchanges throughout the United States were closed, following the example of European stock exchanges. Ship insurance soared to prohibitive figures. Reservists of the French and German armies living outside of their native land were called to the colors and their homeward rush still further

ITALY'S TITANIC LABOR TO CONQUER THE ALPS

When the Italians were making their first mighty advance against Austria descriptions came through of the almost unbelievable natural obstacles they were conquering. Getting one of the monster guns into position in the mountains, as shown above, over the track that had to be built for every foot of its progress, was one such handicap.

THE HISTORIC LANDING FROM THE "RIVER CLYDE" AT SEDDUL BAHR

An incident of the Dardanelles Expedition. Horrible losses were sustained by the Allied troops from the concentrated fire of the Turkish machine guns on shore.

British Official Photograph

BELGIAN SOVEREIGNS RE-ENTER BRUGES

King Albert and Queen Elizabeth of Belgium saluting the Allied colors, on their triumphal entry into Bruges at the head of their victorious army, October 23, 1918.

SURRENDER OF THE GERMAN HIGH SEAS FLEET

Actual photograph showing the greatest naval surrender in history—the German fleet arriving to surrender. *Below,* The commanders of the British and American fleets, Admirals Beatty and Rodman, the King of England and the Prince of Wales viewing the surrender.

"HAIL COLUMBIA"

England greets the first America destroyer squadron to arrive in European waters after the United States entered the war. The British admiral asked Admiral Sims, who was in command, how long he needed to refit and get ready for action. He replied "we are ready now."

THE DAY'S WORK OF UNCLE SAM'S DESTROYERS

More than 2,000,000 men were safely landed in France guarded by the destroyers, ready day or night whenever an enemy submarine threatened a convoy, as was the case here in a trip over of the *Adriatic* loaded with troops. In the foreground is the periscope of the attacking submarine trying to submerge before she is hit.

THE CATHEDRAL OF RHEIMS

In the first weeks of the war the Germans occupied Rheims, but were driven out after von Kluck's retreat. On September 20, 1914, they were reported as first shelling the Cathedral of Rheims and the civilized world stood aghast, for the edifice, begun in 1212, is one of the chief glories of Gothic architecture in all Europe.

Photo by Underwood & Underwood, N. Y.   THE KAISER AND HIS SIX SONS

The ex-Emperor and his sons leading a procession in Berlin soon after the declaration of war. It was noted that in spite of their martial appearance the royal family were extremely careful to keep out of range of the Allied guns. From left to right they are: The Kaiser, Crown Prince Wilhelm, Princes Eitel Friedrich, Adalbert, August, Oscar and Joachim.

CHAPTER III

WHY THE WORLD WENT TO WAR

WHILE it is true that the war was conceived in Berlin, it is none the less true that it was born in the Balkans. It is necessary in order that we may view with correct perspective the background of the World War, that we gain some notion of the Balkan States and the complications entering into their relations. These countries have been the adopted children of the great European powers during generations of rulers. Russia assumed guardianship of the nations having a preponderance of Slavic blood; Roumania with its Latin consanguinities was close to France and Italy; Bulgaria, Greece, and Balkan Turkey were debatable regions wherein the diplomats of the rival nations secured temporary victories by devious methods.

The Balkans have fierce hatreds and have been the site of sudden historic wars. At the time of the declaration of the World War, the Balkan nations were living under the provisions of the Treaty of Bucharest, dated August 10, 1913. Greece, Roumania, Bulgaria, Serbia and Montenegro were signers, and Turkey acquiesced in its provisions.

The assassination at Sarajevo had sent a convulsive shudder throughout the Balkans. The reason lay in the century-old antagonism between the Slav and the Teuton. Serbia, Montenegro and Russia had never forgiven Austria for seizing Bosnia and Herzegovina and making these Slavic people subjects of the Austrian crown. Bulgaria, Roumania and Turkey remained cold at the news of the assassination. German diplomacy was in the ascendant at these courts and the prospect of war with Germany as their great ally presented no terrors for them. The sympathies of the people of Greece were with Serbia, but the Grecian Court, because the Queen of Greece was the only sister of the German Kaiser, was whole heartedly with Austria. Perhaps at the first the Roumanians were most nearly neutral. They believed strongly that each of the small nations of the Balkan region as well as all of the small nations that had been absorbed but had not been digested by Austria, should cut itself from the leading strings held by the large European powers.   There was a distinct undercurrent for a federation resembling that of the United States of America

EUROPE AFTER THE BALKAN WARS

between these peoples.   This was expressed most clearly by M. Jonesco, leader of the Liberal party of Roumania and generally recognized as the ablest statesman of middle Europe.   He declared:

"I always believed, and still believe, that the Balkan States cannot secure their future otherwise than by a close understanding

CHAPTER IV

THE PLOTTER BEHIND THE SCENE

ONE factor alone caused the great war. It was not the assassination at Sarajevo, not the Slavic ferment of anti-Teutonism in Austria and the Balkans. The only cause of the world's greatest war was the determination of the German High Command and the powerful circle surrounding it that "*Der Tag*" had arrived. The assassination at Sarajevo was only the peg for the pendant of war. Another peg would have been found inevitably had not the projection of that assassination presented itself as the excuse.

Germany's military machine was ready. A gray-green uniform that at a distance would fade into misty obscurity had been devised after exhaustive experiments by optical, dye and cloth experts co-operating with the military high command. These uniforms had been standardized and fitted for the millions of men enrolled in Germany's regular and reserve armies. Rifles, great pyramids of munitions, field kitchens, traveling post-offices, motor lorries, a network of military railways leading to the French and Belgian border, all these and more had been made ready. German soldiers had received instructions which enabled each man at a signal to go to an appointed place where he found everything in readiness for his long forced marches into the territory of Germany's neighbors.

More than all this, Germany's spy system, the most elaborate and unscrupulous in the history of mankind, had enabled the German High Command to construct in advance of the declaration of war concrete gun emplacements in Belgium and other invaded territory. The cellars of dwellings and shops rented or owned by German spies were camouflaged concrete foundations for the great guns of Austria and Germany. These emplacements were in exactly the right position for use against the fortresses of Germany's foes. Advertisements and shop-signs were used by spies as guides for the marching German armies of invasion.

In brief, Germany had planned for war. She was approximately ready for it. Under the shelter of such high-sounding phrases as "We demand our place in the sun," and "The seas must be free," the German people were educated into the belief that the hour of Germany's destiny was at hand.

PARTITION OF AFRICA PRIOR TO 1914

German psychologists, like other German scientists, had co-operated with the imperial militaristic government for many years to bring the Germanic mind into a condition of docility. So well did they understand the mentality and the trends of character of the German people that it was comparatively easy to impose upon them a militaristic system and philosophy by which the individual yielded countless personal liberties for the alleged good of the state. Rigorous and compulsory military service,

THE AMERICAN COMMANDER-IN-CHIEF IN THE FIELD

Photograph of General John J. Pershing just after he had been decorated with the Star and Ribbon of the Legion of Honor of France, the highest decoration ever awarded an American soldier. General Pershing was raised to a full generalship soon after his arrival in France, an honor which has previously been held only by Washington, Grant, Sherman and Sheridan.

NOTED AMERICAN GENERALS

General March is chief of staff of the American Army, Lieutenant-Generals Liggett and Bullard commanded the First and Second Armies respectively, and major-generals Wright and Read are corps commanders.

AMMUNITION FOR THE GUNS
Canadian narrow-gauge line taking ammunition up the line through a
shattered village.

HOW VERDUN WAS SAVED
The motor transport never faltered when the railroads were put out of action.

CAPTAIN CHARLES A. FRYATT

The martyred British Merchant-Marine Captain, who was executed by the Germans because his ship attempted to sink a German submarine which attacked her.

NURSE EDITH CAVELL

A victim of German savagery. An English lady whose life had been devoted to works of mercy, was shot after summary trial, at Brussels on October 11, 1915, for helping British and Belgian fugitives.

"TIME'S UP! OVER YOU GO!"

The word comes from the officer, watch in hand, "Time's up! Over you go!" and instantly the men from the Dominion begin to climb out of the trench. The picture shows the departure of the first of the three or more lines or "waves" that moves forward over "No Man's Land" against the enemy trenches.

Photo by International Film Service.

TRANSPORTING WOUNDED AMID THE DIFFICULTIES OF THE ITALIAN MOUNTAIN FRONT

The isolated mountain positions were only accessible to the bases of operations by these aerial cable cars. This picture, taken during the Austrian retreat, shows a wounded soldier being taken down the mountain by this means.

© *Underwood and Underwood, N. Y.* *British Official Photo*

THE NERVE-SYSTEM OF THE FIGHTING ARMIES

What the nerves are to the human body the signal system was to the armies, transmitting warnings of danger from the outposts to a central brain, and flashing back the thing to be done to meet it.

British Official Photo

FORWARD WITH THE TANKS AGAINST BAPAUME

This picture gives an excellent idea of the method of combined tank and infantry attack. Behind a low ridge among artillery positions they are forming their line. A company falls in behind one of the waddling monsters that will break a way for it through all obstacles, while on both sides of the road other detachments await the arrival of the tank they are to accompany.

Canadian Official Photograph   *From Underwood & Underwood, N. Y.*

CANADIANS IN THE GREAT CAMBRAI DRIVE

One of the busy scenes just preceding the victorious attack by the Canadians upon Cambrai. In the center can be seen captured Germans carrying in one of their wounded comrades.

CHAPTER V

THE GREAT WAR BEGINS

YEARS before 1914, when Germany declared war against civilization, it was decided by the German General Staff to strike at France through Belgium. The records of the German Foreign Office prove that fact. The reason for this lay in the long line of powerful fortresses along the line that divides France from Germany and the sparsely spaced and comparatively out-of-date forts on the border between Germany and Belgium. True, there was a treaty guaranteeing the inviolability of Belgian territory to which Germany was a signatory party. Some of the clauses of that treaty were:

"Article 9. Belgium, within the limits traced in conformity with the principles laid down in the present preliminaries, shall form a perpetually neutral state. The five powers (England, France, Austria, Prussia and Russia), without wishing to intervene in the internal affairs of Belgium, guarantee her that perpetual neutrality as well as the integrity and inviolability of her territory in the limits mentioned in the present article.

"Article 10. By just reciprocity Belgium shall be held to observe this same neutrality toward all the other states and to make no attack on their internal or external tranquillity while always preserving the right to defend herself against any foreign aggression."

This agreement was followed on January 23, 1839, by a definitive treaty, accepted by Belgium and by the Netherlands, which treaty regulates Belgium's neutrality as follows:

"Article 7. Belgium, within the limits defined in Articles 1, 2 and 4, shall form an independent and perpetually neutral state. She is obligated to preserve this neutrality against all the other states."

To convert this solemn covenant into a "scrap of paper" it was necessary that Germany should find an excuse for tearing it to pieces. There was absolutely no provocation in sight, but that

77

did not deter the German High Command. That august body with no information whatever to afford an excuse, alleged in a formal note to the Belgian Government that the French army intended to invade Germany through Belgian territory. This hypocritical and mendacious note and Belgium's vigorous reply follow:

Note handed in on August 2, 1914, at 7 o'clock P. M., by Herr von Below-Saleske, German Minister, to M. Davignon, Belgian Minister for Foreign Affairs.

BRUSSELS, 2d August, 1914.

Imperial German Legation in Belgium.

(Highly confidential.)

The German Government has received reliable information according to which the French forces intend to march on the Meuse, by way of Givet and Namur. This information leaves no doubt as to the intention of France of marching on Germany through Belgian territory. The Imperial German Government cannot avoid the fear that Belgium, in spite of its best will, will be in no position to repulse such a largely developed French march without aid. In this fact there is sufficient certainty of a threat directed against Germany.

It is an imperative duty for the preservation of Germany to forestall this attack of the enemy.

The German Government would feel keen regret if Belgium should regard as an act of hostility against herself the fact that the measures of the enemies of Germany oblige her on her part to violate Belgian territory.

In order to dissipate any misunderstanding the German Government declares as follows:

1. Germany does not contemplate any act of hostility against Belgium. If Belgium consents in the war about to commence to take up an attitude of friendly neutrality toward Germany, the German Government on its part undertakes, on the declaration of peace, to guarantee the kingdom and its possessions in their whole extent.

2. Germany undertakes under the conditions laid down to evacuate Belgian territory as soon as peace is concluded.

3. If Belgium preserves a friendly attitude, Germany is prepared, in agreement with the authorities of the Belgian Government, to buy against cash all that is required by her troops, and to give indemnity for the damages caused in Belgium.

4. If Belgium behaves in a hostile manner toward the German troops, and in particular raises difficulties against their advance by the opposition of the fortifications of the Meuse, or by destroying roads, railways, tunnels, or other engineering works, Germany will be compelled to consider Belgium as an enemy.

In this case Germany will take no engagements toward Belgium, but she will leave the later settlement of relations of the two states

WHERE THE WORLD WAR BEGAN.

CHAPTER VI

THE TRAIL OF THE BEAST IN BELGIUM

GERMANY'S onrush into heroic Belgium speedily resolved itself into a saturnalia that drenched the land with blood and roused the civilized world into resentful horror. As the tide of barbarity swept forward into Northern France, stories of the horrors filtered through the close web of German censorship. There were denials at first by German propagandists. In the face of truth furnished by thousands of witnesses, the denials faded away.

What caused these atrocities? Were they the spontaneous expression of dormant brutishness in German soldiers? Were they a sudden reversion of an entire nation to bestiality?

The answer is that the private soldier as an individual was not responsible. The carnage, the rapine, the wholesale desolation was an integral part of the German policy of *schrecklichkeit* or frightfulness. This policy was laid down by Germany as part of its imperial war code. In 1902 Germany issued a new war manual entitled "Kriegsbrauch im Landkriege." In it is written this cold-blooded declaration:

> All measures which conduce to the attainment of the object of war are permissible and these may be summarized in the two ideas of violence and cunning. What is permissible includes every means of war without which the object of the war cannot be attained. All means which modern invention affords, including the fullest, most dangerous, and most massive means of destruction, may be utilized.

Brand Whitlock, United States Minister to Belgium, in a formal report to the State Department, made this statement concerning Germany's policy in permitting these outrages:

"All these deliberate organized massacres of civilians, all these murders and outrages, the violation of women, the killing of children, wanton destruction, burning, looting and pillage, and whole towns destroyed, were acts for which no possible military necessity can be pleaded. They were wilfully committed as part

90

of a deliberately prepared and scientifically organized policy of terrorism."

And now, having considered these outrages as part of German policy of terrorism, let us turn to the facts presented by those who made investigations at first hand in devastated Belgium and Northern France.

Let us first turn to the tragic story of the destruction of Louvain. The first document comes in the form of a cable sent from the Belgian Minister of Foreign Affairs under date of August 8, 1914:

"On Tuesday evening a body of German troops who had been driven back retired in disorder upon the town of Louvain. Germans who were guarding the town thought that the retiring troops were Belgians and fired upon them. In order to excuse this mistake the Germans, in spite of the most energetic denials on the part of the authorities, pretended that Belgians had fired on the Germans, although all the inhabitants, including policemen, had been disarmed for more than a week. Without any examination and without listening to any protest the commanding officer announced that the town would be immediately destroyed. All inhabitants had to leave their homes at once; some were made prisoners; women and children were put into a train of which the destination was unknown; soldiers with fire bombs set fire to the different quarters of the town; the splendid Church of St. Pierre, the markets, the university and its scientific establishments, were given to the flames, and it is probable that the Hotel de Ville, this celebrated jewel of Gothic art, will also have disappeared in the disaster. Several notabilities were shot at sight. Thus a town of 40,000 inhabitants, which, since the fifteenth century, has been the intellectual and scientific capital of the Low Countries is a heap of ashes. Americans, many of whom have followed the course at this illustrious alma mater and have there received such cordial hospitality, cannot remain insensible to this outrage on the rights of humanity and civilization which is unprecedented in history."

Minister Whitlock made the following report on the same outrage:

"A violent fusillade broke out simultaneously at various points in the city (Louvain), notably at the Porte de Bruxelles,

CHAPTER IX

CAMPAIGN IN THE EAST

LONG before the declaration of war the German military experts had made their plans. They recognized that in case of war with Russia, France would come to the rescue of its ally. They hoped that Italy, and felt sure that England, would remain neutral, but, no doubt, had provided for the possibility that these two nations would join the ranks of their foes. They recognized that they would be compelled to fight against greatly superior numbers, but they had this advantage, that they were prepared to move at once, while England was unprepared, and Russia, with enormous numbers, was so unprovided with railroad facilities that it would take weeks before her armies would be dangerous.

Their plan of campaign, then, was obvious. Leaving in the East only such forces as were necessary for a strong defense, they would throw the bulk of their strength against the French. They anticipated an easy march to Paris, and then with France at their mercy they would gather together all their powers and deal with Russia. But they had underestimated both the French power of resistance, and the Russian weakness, and in particular they had not counted upon the check that they were to meet with in gallant Belgium.

The Russian mobilization was quicker by far than had been anticipated. Her armies were soon engaged with the comparatively small German forces, and met with great success.

To understand the Russian campaign one must have some knowledge of the geography of western Russia. Russian Poland projects as a great quadrilateral into eastern Germany. It is bounded on the north by East Prussia, on the south by Galicia, and the western part reaches deep into Germany itself. The land is a broad, level plain, through which from south to north runs the River Vistula. In the center lies the capital, Warsaw, protected by a group of fortresses. The Russian army, therefore,

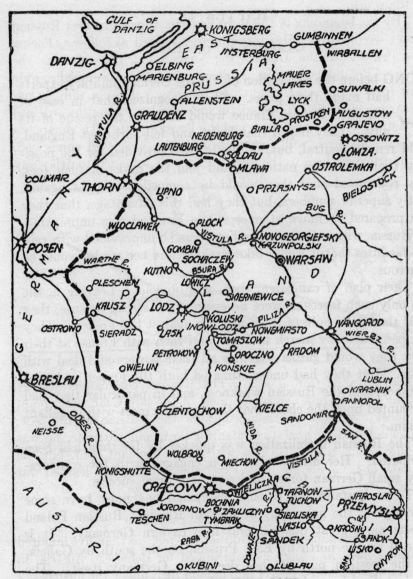

THE EASTERN FIGHTING ZONE.

could not make a direct western advance until it had protected its flanks by the conquest of East Prussia on the north, and Galicia on the south.

By the beginning of the third week in August the first Russian armies were ready. Her forces were arranged as follows: Facing East Prussia was the Army of the Niemen, four corps strong; the Army of Poland, consisting of fifteen army corps, occupied a wide front from Narev on the north to the Bug Valley; a third army, the Army of Galicia, directed its line of advance southward into the country between Lemberg and the River Sareth. The fortresses protecting Warsaw, still further to the east, were well garrisoned, and in front of them to the west were troops intended to delay any

THE SWEEP OF GERMAN ARMIES

German advance from Posen. The Russian commander-in-chief was the Grand Duke Nicholas, uncle of the late Czar, and one of the most admirable representatives of the Russian at his best; a splendid soldier, honest, straightforward, and patriotic, he was the idol of his men. He had with him a brilliant staff, but the strength of his army lay in its experience. They had learned war in the bitter school of the Manchurian campaign.

THE FORCES ON THE FRONTIER

The German force on the frontier was not less than five hundred thousand men, and they were arranged for defense. Austria, in Galicia, had gathered nearly one million men under the auspices of Frederick. The first movement of these armies took place in East Prussia. The Army of the Niemen had completed its mobilization early in August, and was under the command of General Rennen-

STORMING THE MOLE AT ZEEBRUGGE

One of the most brilliant and spectacular feats in naval history was the British blocking of the submarine harbor at Zeebrugge. The picture shows one of the detachments of marines that braved the terrific German defense fire and swarmed up the mole that protects the harbor, planting explosives that made a great breach and let the tides in.

ITALIAN TROOPS TREKKING THE SNOW-FIELDS OF THE ALPS

The Alpine troops of the Italian army have for years developed a military technique peculiar to the regions they must cover. Here a battalion of Alpini is seen on skis, the best method for traveling over the frozen snow crusts of the mountain region.

THE USEFUL ROLE OF THE CARRIER PIGEON AT THE FRONT

No one would think of giving a Distinguished Service Medal to a pigeon, but some of them performed service under fire that would have entitled a soldier to it. Here American officers heading a division are attaching a message to a pigeon in front of the headquarters dugout.

MANY-STORIED BAGDAD FALLS TO THE BRITISH

General Maude is here shown making his formal entry at the head of his troops into the Turkish city. This occurred on March 11, 1917, and was the most notable exploit of General Maude, commander of the British Mesopotamian expedition until his death by cholera nine months afterwards.

ON VIMY RIDGE, WHERE CANADA WON LAURELS

The Canadians took the important position of Vimy Ridge on Easter Monday, April 9, 1917. They advanced with brilliance, having taken the whole system of German front-line trenches between dawn and 6.30 A. M. This shows squads of machine gunners operating from shell-craters in support of the infantry on the plateau above the ridge.

GENERAL ARTHUR CURRIE
Commander of the Canadian forces on the Western Front

WOODROW WILSON

President of the United States during the whole course of the war and Commander-in-Chief of its army and navy. On November 11, 1918, he signalized the end of the war in a proclamation in which he said:—"My Fellow-Countrymen:—The armistice was signed this morning. Everything for which America fought has been accomplished."

WHEN IT WAS OVER "OVER THERE"

Victorious American troops arriving at New York after the signing of the armistice.

CHAPTER X

The Struggle for Supremacy on the Sea

CAPTAIN MAHAN'S thesis that in any great war the nation possessing the greater sea power is likely to win, has been splendidly illustrated during the present war. The great English fleets have been the insuperable obstacle to the ambitious German plans of world dominion. The millions of soldiers landed in France from Great Britain, and its provinces, the millions of Americans transported in safety across the water, and the enormous quantities of supplies put at the disposal of the Allies depended, absolutely, upon the Allied control of the sea routes of the world. With a superior navy a German blockade of England would have brought her to terms in a short period, and France, left to fight alone, would have been an easy victim. The British navy has saved the world.

Germany had for many years well understood the necessity of power upon the sea. When the war broke out it was the second greatest of the sea powers. Its ships were mostly modern, for its navy was a creation of the past fifteen years, and its development was obviously for the purpose of attacking the British supremacy. The father of this new navy was a naval officer by the name of von Tirpitz, who, in 1897, had become the German Naval Minister. With the aid of the Emperor he had aroused among the Germans a great enthusiasm for maritime power, and had built up a navy in fifteen years, which was second only to the English navy.

Von Tirpitz was an interesting character. In appearance he looked like an old sea-wolf who had passed his life on the wave, but such a thought would be a mistake. The great admiral has done his work on land; he is an organizer, a diplomatist, a politician. He has created nothing new; in all its details he has copied the English fleet. He is tall, heavily built, with a great white beard, forked in the middle. He is a man of much dignity, with a smile which has won him renown. He might have been Chancellor of the Empire, but he preferred to devote himself to

145

the navy, to prove that the future of Germany is on the seas. His glories are the Lusitania, the fleet safely anchored at Kiel, and the long rows of innocent victims of the submarine.

He was born in 1850 at Kustrion on the Ildor, when the German navy was only a little group of worthless boats. In 1865 he entered the School of Cadets, in 1869 he was gazetted lieutenant, in 1875 he was lieutenant-commander with a reputation as an able organizer. In 1891 he was appointed Chief of Staff at Kiel. This was his opportunity, and he set himself at the task of creating and protecting the submarine division of the navy. As time went on he grew in importance. In 1898 he became Assistant Secretary

ENGLISH COAST TOWNS THAT WERE RAIDED

of State at the Admiralty in Berlin. Two years later he became vice-admiral. His admirers recognized his powers, and he was called the master. In 1899 a patent of nobility was conferred upon him. In 1902 he gained permission to build 13,000-ton war ships, and the following year he was made admiral. In 1907 enormous appropriations were made at his desire for the enlargement of the fleet. In 1908 Emperor William conferred on him the Order of the Black Eagle. In 1914 the Kiel Canal was completed under his direction, and he informed the Emperor that the fleet was ready. It is only fair to add that in all his plans he had the active support of his Imperial Master. The Kaiser, too, had dreamed a dream. Von Tirpitz admired the English. His children had been brought up in England, as was also his wife.

CHAPTER XI

THE SUBLIME PORTE

AS SOON as the diplomatic relations between Austria and Serbia had been broken, the Turkish Grand Vizier informed the diplomatic corps in Constantinople that Turkey would remain neutral in the conflict. The declaration was not formal, for war had not yet been declared. The policy of Turkey, as represented in the ministerial paper, *Tasfiri-Efkiar*, was as follows:

"Turkey has never asked for war, as she always has worked toward avoiding it, but neutrality does not mean indifference. The present Austro-Serbian conflict is to a supreme degree interesting to us. In the first place, one of our erstwhile opponents is fighting against a much stronger enemy. In the natural course of things Serbia, which till lately was expressing, in a rather open way, her solidarity as a nation, still provoking us, and Greece, will be materially weakened. In the second place, the results of this war may surpass the limits of the conflict between two countries, and in that case our interests will be just as materially affected. We must, therefore, keep our eyes open, as the circumstances are momentarily changing, and do not permit us to let escape certain advantages which we can secure by active, and rightly acting, diplomacy. The policy of neutrality will impose on us the obligation of avoiding to side with either of the belligerents. But the same policy will force us to take all the necessary measures, for safeguarding our interests and our frontiers."

Whereupon a Turkish mobilization was at once ordered. The war had hardly begun when Turkey received the news that her two battleships, building in British yards, had been taken over by England. A bitter feeling against England was at once aroused, Turkish mobs proceeded to attack the British stores and British subjects, and attempts were even made against the British embassy in Constantinople, and the British consulate at Smyrna.

At this time Turkey was in a peculiar position. For a cen-

WHERE TURKEY ONCE REIGNED SUPREME.

tury she had been on the best of terms with France and Great
Britain. On the other hand Russia had been her hereditary enemy.
She was still suffering from her defeat by the Balkan powers, and
her statesmen saw in this war great possibilities. She desired to
recover her lost provinces in Europe, and saw at once that she
could hope for little from the Allies in this direction.

For some years, too, German intrigues, and, according to
report, German money, had enabled the German Government to
control the leading Turkish statesmen. German generals, under

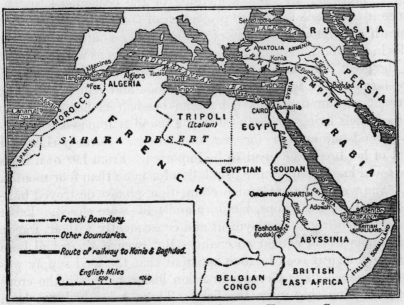

STRETCHES OF COUNTRY THAT THE GERMANS HOPED TO CONTROL

General Liman von Sanders, were practically in control of the
Turkish army. The commander-in-chief was Enver Bey, who had
been educated in Germany and was more German than the Germans.
A new system of organization for the Turkish army had been
established by the Germans, which had substituted the mechanical
German system for the rough and inefficient Turkish methods.
Universal conscription provided men, and the Turkish soldier has
always been known as a good soldier. Yet as it turned out the
German training did little for him. Under his own officers he
could fight well, but under German officers, fighting for a cause
which he neither liked nor understood, he was bound to fail.

CHAPTER XII

RESCUE OF THE STARVING

THE sufferings of Belgium during the German occupation were terrible, and attracted the attention and the sympathy of the whole world. To understand conditions it is necessary to know something of the economic situation. Since it had come under the protection of the Great Powers, Belgium had developed into one of the greatest manufacturing countries in the world. Nearly two million of her citizens were employed in the great industries, and one million two hundred thousand on the farms. She was peaceful, industrious and happy. But on account of the fact that more than one-half of her citizenship earned their living by daily labor she found it impossible to produce foodstuff enough for her own needs. Seventy-eight per cent of her breadstuffs had to be imported. From her own fields she could hardly supply her population for more than four months.

The war, and the German occupation, almost destroyed business. Mines, workshops, factories and mills were closed. Labor found itself without employment and consequently without wages. The banks would extend no credit. But even if there had been money enough it soon became apparent that the food supply was rapidly going. The German invasion had come when the crops were standing ripe upon the field. Those crops had not been reaped, but had been trampled under foot by the hated German.

One feature of Belgian industrial life should be understood. Hundreds of thousands of her workmen were employed each day in workshops at considerable distances from their own homes. In times of peace the morning and evening trains were always crowded with laborers going to and returning from their daily toil. One of the first things seized upon by the German officials was the railroads, and it was with great difficulty that anyone, not belonging to the German army, could obtain an opportunity to travel at all, and it was with still greater difficulty that supplies of food of any kind could be transported from place to place.

Every village was cut off from its neighbor, every town from the next town. People were unable even to obtain news of the great political events which were occurring from day to day, and the food supply was automatically cut off.

But this was not the worst. One of the first moves of the German occupation was to quarter hundreds of thousands of troops upon their Belgian victims, and these troops must be fed even though the Belgian and his family were near starvation. Then followed the German seizure of what they called materials for war. General von Beseler in a despatch to the Kaiser, after the fall of Antwerp, speaks very plainly:

> The war booty taken at Antwerp is enormous,—at least five hundred cannon and huge quantities of ammunition, sanitation materials, high power motor cars, locomotives, wagons, four million kilograms of wheat, large quantities of flour, coal and flax wool, the value of which is estimated at ten million marks, copper, silver, one armored train, several hospital trains, and quantities of fish.

The Germans proceeded to commandeer foodstuffs and raw materials of industry. Linseed oil, oil cakes, nitrates, animal and vegetable oils, petroleum and mineral oils, wool, copper, rubber, ivory, cocoa, rice, wine, beer, all were seized and sent home to the Fatherland. Moreover, cities and provinces were burdened with formidable war contributions. Brussels was obliged to pay ten million dollars, Antwerp ten million dollars, the province of Brabant, ninety millions of dollars, Namur and seventeen surrounding communes six million four hundred thousand dollars. Finally Governor von Bissing, on the 10th of December, 1914, issued the following decree:

> A war contribution of the amount of eight million dollars to be paid monthly for one year is imposed upon the population of Belgium. The payment of these amounts is imposed upon the nine provinces which are regarded as joint debtors. The two first monthly payments are to be made by the 15th of January, 1915, at latest, and the following monthly payments by the tenth of each following month to the military chest of the Field Army of the General Imperial Government in Brussels. If the provinces are obliged to resort to the issue of stock with a view to procuring the necessary funds, the form and terms of these shares will be determined by the Commissary General for the banks in Belgium.

At a meeting of the Provincial Councils the vice-president declared: "The Germans demand these $96,000,000 of the country without right and without reason. Are we to sanction this enormous war tax? If we listened only to our hearts, we should reply 'No! ninety-six million times no!' because our hearts would tell us we were a small, honest nation living happily by its free labor; we were a small, honest nation having faith in treaties and believing in honor; we were a nation unarmed, but full of confidence, when Germany suddenly hurled two million men upon our frontiers, the most brutal army that the world has ever seen, and said to us, 'Betray the promise you have given. Let my armies go by, that I may crush France, and I will give you gold.' Belgium replied, 'Keep your gold. I prefer to die, rather than live without honor.' The German army has, therefore, crushed our country in contempt of solemn treaties. 'It is an injustice,' said the Chancellor of the German Empire. 'The position of Germany has forced us to commit it, but we will repair the wrong we have done to Belgium by the passage of our armies.' They want to repair the injustice as follows: Belgium will pay Germany $96,000,000! Give this proposal your vote. When Galileo had discovered the fact that the earth moved around the sun, he was forced at the foot of the stake to abjure his error, but he murmured, 'Nevertheless it moves.' Well, gentlemen, as I fear a still greater misfortune for my country I consent to the payment of the $96,000,000 and I cry 'Nevertheless it moves.' Long live our country in spite of all."

TOLLS TO THE TEUTON

At the end of a year von Bissing renewed this assessment, inserting in his decree the statement that the decree was based upon article forty-nine of The Hague Convention, relating to the laws and usages of war on land. This article reads as follows: "If in addition to the taxes mentioned in the above article the occupant levies other moneyed contributions in the occupied territory, they shall only be applied to the needs of the army, or of the administration, of the territory in question." In the preceding article it says: "If in the territory occupied the occupant collects the taxes, dues and tolls payable to the state, he shall do so as far as possible in accordance with the legal basis and assessment in force at the time, and shall in consequence be bound to defray the expenses of the administration of the occupied territories to

CHATEAU-THIERRY, WHERE AMERICA INFLICTED A SECOND GETTYSBURG ON GERMANY

Poilus and Yanks in the foreground looking over the roofs of Châteu-Thierry, where in the middle of July in the last year of the war, the Americans at a crucial moment stopped the German advance in the second battle of the Marne. After that Germany never went forward on any field of battle again.

French Official Photograph by International Film Service.

WIPING OUT THE ST. MIHIEL SALIENT

The first major exploit carried out independently by the American army was the obliteration of the St. Mihiel salient, which had been in German hands since 1914 in two days, a spectacular achievement, carried out with great brilliance and precision. The picture shows U. S. troops following the Germans through Thiaucourt, one of the towns on the salient.

WOMEN AT WORK THAT MEN MAY FIGHT

The women of the world took up, quickly almost every masculine task in industry to release their menfolk for the firing line. They were especially valuable in the munitions factories of England, as shown above. The women in the foreground are testing shell cases for size, while those in the background work the lathes.

A BELGIAN MILITARY OBSERVATION BALLOON

Large numbers of these balloons, which came to be known as sausages, were used by the Allied armies on all fronts.

THE FINAL TRIBUTE

Allied airman dropping a wreath on the grave of a comrade who fell and was buried within the German lines.

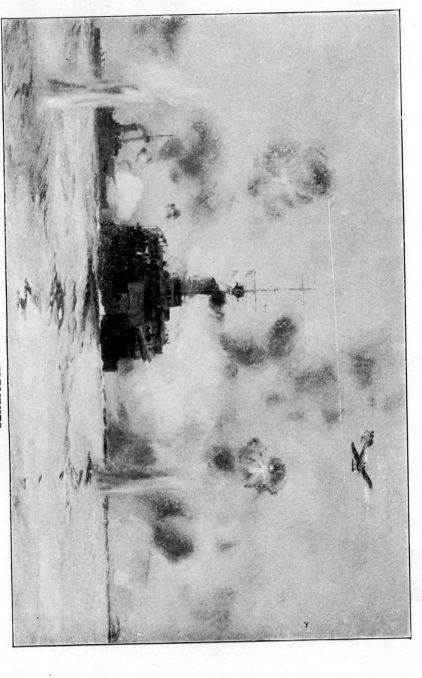

A BATTLE OF FOUR ELEMENTS

British monitors shelling the German land batteries near Nieuport. German submarines were actively engaged in trying to torpedo these monitors and the British monoplane was useful for giving the range to the ship and reporting the accuracy of the shots.

TORPEDOING OF THE BRITISH BATTLESHIP, "ABOUKIR"

In the first few weeks of the war, when the navies of the world were
still at open warfare, during a sharp engagement off the Hook of Holland
in the North Sea the British warships "Aboukir", "Cressy" and "Hogue"
fell victims to the enemy. This sketch shows the "Aboukir" after a German
torpedo had found its mark in her hull.

BULGARIANS CELEBRATE PEACE

The first peace picture.   The Bulgarian army is holding a solemn thanksgiving mass on the battle field just after the signing of the armistice which ended their participation in the war.

AMERICAN COLORED SOLDIERS IN ALSACE

French Official Photograph

Inspection of arms before going into action. Colored troops were in battles with the Germans many times and succeeded in beating the enemy in every instance.

the same extent as the National Government had been so bound."

The $96,000,000 per annum was more than six times the amount of the direct taxes formerly collected by the Belgian state, taxes which the German administration, moreover, collected in addition to the war assessment. It was five times as great as the ordinary expenditure of the Belgian War Department.

A Contour Map of the Western Front

But this was not all. In addition to the more or less legitimate German methods of plunder the whole country had been pillaged. In many towns systematic pillage began as soon as the Germans took possession. At Louvain the pillage began on the 27th of August, 1914, and lasted a week. In small bands the soldiers went from house to house, ransacked drawers and cupboards, broke open safes, and stole money, pictures, curios, silver, linen,

CHAPTER XIII

BRITANNIA RULES THE WAVES

THE month of October, 1914, contained no important naval contests. On the 15th, the old British cruiser Hawke was torpedoed in the North Sea and nearly five hundred men were lost. On the other hand, on the 17th of October, the light cruiser Undaunted, accompanied by the destroyers, Lance, Legion and Loyal, sank four German destroyers off the Dutch coast. But the opening of November turned the interest of the navy to the Southern Pacific. When the war began Admiral von Spee, with the German Pacific squadron, was at Kiaochau in command of seven vessels. Among these was the Emden, whose adventurous career has been already described. Another, the Karlsruhe, became a privateer in the South Atlantic.

Early in August Von Spee set sail from Kiaochau with two armored cruisers, the Gneisenau and the Scharnhorst and three light cruisers, the Dresden, Leipzig and Nurmberg. These ships were comparatively new, well armed, and of considerable speed. They set off for the great trade highways to destroy, as far as possible, British commerce. Their route led them to the western coast of South America, and arrangements were made so that they were coaled and provisioned from bases in some of the South American states which permitted a slack observance of the laws respecting the duties of neutrals.

A small British squadron had been detailed to protect British commerce in this part of the world. It was commanded by Rear Admiral Sir Christopher Cradock, a distinguished and popular sailor, who had under his command one twelve-year-old battleship, the Canopus, two armored cruisers, the Good Hope and the Monmouth, the light cruiser Glasgow, and an armed liner, the Otranto. None of these vessels had either great speed or heavy armament. The equipment of the Canopus, indeed, was obsolete. Admiral Cradock's squadron arrived at Halifax on August 14th, thence sailed to Bermuda, then on past Venezuela and Brazil

around the Horn. It visited the Falkland Islands, and by the
third week of October was on the coast of Chile. The Canopus had
dropped behind for repairs, and though reinforcements were
expected, they had not yet arrived. They knew that their force
was inferior to that of Admiral von Spee.

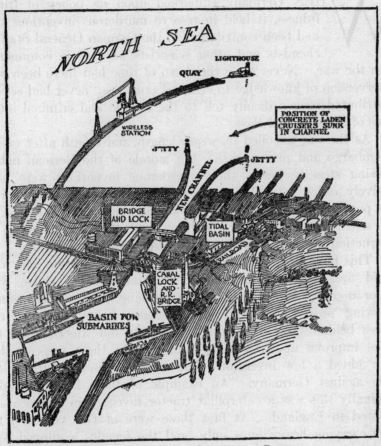

ZEEBRUGGE HARBOR, BLOCKED BY BRITISH

One officer wrote, on the 12th of October, "From now till the
end of the month is the critical time, as it will decide whether we
shall have to fight a superior German force from the Pacific before
we can get reinforcements from home or the Mediterranean. We
feel that the admiralty ought to have a better force here, but we
shall fight cheerfully whatever odds we have to face."

CHAPTER XIV

New Methods and Horrors of Warfare

WHEN Germany embarked upon its policy of frightfulness, it held in reserve murderous inventions that had been contributed to the German General Staff by chemists and other scientists working in conjunction with the war. Never since the dawn of time had there been such a perversion of knowledge to criminal purposes; never had science contributed such a deadly toll to the fanatic and criminal intentions of a war-crazed class.

As the war uncoiled its weary length, and month after month of embargo and privation saw the morale of the German nation growing steadily lower, these murderous inventions were successively called into play against the Allies, but as each horror was put into play on the battle-field, its principles were solved by the scientists of the Allied nations, and the deadly engine of destruction was turned with trebled force against the Huns.

This happened with the various varieties of poison gas, with liquid fire, with trench knives, with nail-studded clubs, with armor used by shock troops, with airplane bombs, with cannon throwing projectiles weighing thousands of pounds great distances behind the battle lines. Not only did America and the Allies improve upon Germany's pattern in these respects, but they added a few inventions that went far toward turning the scale against Germany. An example of these is the "tank." Originally this was a caterpillar tractor invented in America and adopted in England. At first these were of two varieties, the male, carrying heavy guns only, and the females, equipped with machine guns. To these was later added the whippet tank, named after the racing dog developed in England. These whippet tanks averaged eighteen miles an hour, carrying death and terror into the ranks of the enemy. All the tanks were heavily armored and had as their motto the significant words "Treat 'Em Rough." The Germans designed a heavy anti-tank rifle about three feet longer than the ordinary rifle and carrying a charge calculated to pierce tank armor. These were issued to the German first line trenches at the rate of three to a company. That they were not particularly effective was proved by the ease with which the tanks of all varieties tore through the barbed wire entanglements and passed over the Hindenburg and Kriemhild lines, supposed by the Germans to be impregnable.

The tanks in effect were mobile artillery and were used as such by all the Allied troops. Germany frantically endeavored to manufacture tanks to meet the Allied monsters, but their efforts were feeble when compared with the great output opposed to them.

CHANGES IN METHODS AND TACTICS NECESSARY

Before considering other inventions used for the first time in this war, it is well to understand the tremendous changes in methods and tactics made necessary by these discoveries.

Put into a sentence, the changed warfare amounts to this: it is a mobilization of material, of railroads, great guns, machine guns, food, airplanes and other engines of destruction quite as much as it is a mobilization of men.

The Germans won battle after battle at the beginning of the war because of their system of strategic railways that made it possible to transport huge armies to selected points in the shortest possible time both on the eastern and the western fronts. Lacking a system of transportation to match this, Russia lost the great battles that decided her fate, Belgium was over-run, and France, once the border was passed, became a battle-field upon which the Germans might extend their trench systems over the face of the land.

Lacking strategic railways to match those of Germany, France evolved an effective substitute in the modern system of automobile transportation. When von Kluck swung aside from Paris in his first great rush, Gallieni sent out from Paris an army in taxicabs that struck the exposed flank and went far toward winning the first battle of the Marne. It was the truck transportation system of the French along the famous "Sacred Road" back of the battle line at Verdun that kept inviolate the motto of the heroic town, "They Shall Not Pass." Motor trucks that brought American reserves in a khaki flood won the second battle of the Marne. It was automobile transportation that enabled Haig to send the British Canadians and Australians in full cry after the retreating Germans when the backbone of the German resistance was broken before Lens, Cambrai, and Ostend.

RAILROADS BUILT BY AMERICANS

America's railway transportation system in France was one of the marvels of the war. Stretching from the sector of seacoast set apart for America by the French Government, it radiated far into the interior, delivering men, munitions and food in a steady stream. American engineers worked with their brothers-in-arms with the Allies to construct an inter-weaving system of wide-gauge and narrow-gauge roads that served to victual and munition the entire front and further serve to deliver at top speed whole army corps. It was this network of strategic railways that enabled the French to send an avalanche clad in horizon blue to the relief of Amiens when Hindenburg made his final tremendous effort of 1918.

In its essentials, military effort in the great conflict may be roughly divided into

Open warfare,
Trench warfare,
Crater warfare.

The first battle of the Marne was almost wholly open warfare; so also were the battles of the Masurian Lakes, Allenstein, and Dunajec in the eastern theater of war, and most of the warfare on the Italian front between the Piave River and Gorizia.

In this variety of battle, airplanes and observation balloons play a prominent part. Once the enemy is driven out of its trenches, the message is flashed by wireless to the artillery and slaughter at long range begins. If there have been no intrenchments, as was the case in the first battle of the Marne, massed artillery send a plunging fire into the columns moving in open order and prepare the way for machine gunners and infantry to finish the rout.

CAVALRY IN THE WAR

In previous wars, cavalry played a heroic rôle in open warfare; only rarely has it been possible to use cavalry in the Great War.

The Germans sent a screen of Uhlans before its advancing hordes into Belgium and Northern France in 1914. The Uhlans also were in the van in the Russian invasion, but with these exceptions, German cavalry has been a negligible factor.

British and French cavalry were active in pursuit of the fleeing Teutons when the Hindenburg line was smashed in

THE COALITION OF GERMAN KINGDOMS

September of 1918. Outside of that brief episode, the cavalry did comparatively nothing so far as the Allies were concerned. It was the practice on both sides to dismount cavalry and convert it into some form of trench service. Trench mortar companies, bombing squads, and other specialty groups were organized from among the cavalrymen. Of course the fighting in the open stretches of Mesopotamia, South Africa and Russia involved the use of great bodies of cavalry. The trend of modern warfare,

CHAPTER XV

German Plots and Propaganda in America

THE pages of Germany's militaristic history are black with many shameful deeds and plots. Those pages upon which are written the intrigues against the peace of America and against the lives and properties of American citizens during the period between the declaration of war in 1914 and the armistice ending the war, while not so bloody as those relating to the atrocities in Belgium and Northern France are still revolting to civilized mankind.

Germany not only paid for the murder of passengers on ships where its infernal machines were placed, not only conspired for the destruction of munition plants and factories of many kinds, not only sought to embroil the United States, then neutral, in a war with Mexico and Japan, but it committed also the crime of murderous hypocrisy by conspiring to do these wrongs under the cloak of friendship for this country.

It was in December of 1915 that the German Government sent to the United States for general publication in American newspapers this statement:

> The German Government has naturally never knowingly accepted the support of any person, group of persons, society or organization seeking to promote the cause of Germany in the United States by illegal acts, by counsel of violence, by contravention of law, or by any means whatever that could offend the American people in the pride of their own authority.

The answer to this imperial lie came from the President of the United States, when, in his address to Congress, April 2, 1917, urging a declaration of war on Germany, he characterized the German spy system and its frightful fruits in the following language:

"One of the things that has served to convince us that the Prussian autocracy was not and could never be our friend is that from the very outset of the present war it has filled our unsuspecting communities, and even our offices of government, with

PICKING ONE "OFF THE TAIL"

The German Albatross aeroplane going down in flames was in pursuit of the light British "Quick" machine seen on the left, when suddenly a British Nieuport (at the right) dived through the clouds. The Albatross nose-dived, the British following with his guns working, and soon the German burst into flames and crashed to earth, his pursuer straightening out his course.

CARRYING THE WAR INTO GERMANY

Mechanics "tuning up" one of the giant British bombing machines developed in 1918 that raided Germany. The size is shown by comparison with the human figures. Note the forward gunner, the pilot, the rear gunner and the window of the commodious cock-pit within which the airmen could stand upright.

THE FURY OF A COSSACK CHARGE

Some of the most bitter fighting of the war took place on the snow-covered heights of the Carpathians when Russia's armies struggled with the foe. Here is illustrated a charge by Cossacks on an Austrian battery. There is nothing in warfare quite like the furious onslaught of the little men of the steppes on their wiry ponies.

HIDE AND SEEK IN THE BALTIC

A Zeppelin flying over a British submarine in the stormy sea.

THE LUSITANIA

The sinking of this great liner by a German submarine, with the loss of more than a thousand lives, caused a thrill of horror throughout all neutral nations and crystallized public opinion in the United States into a fierce resentment of German barbarism which indirectly led to the entry into the World War.

SUBMARINE HUNTING

A small naval dirigible used for scouting by the British Navy.   Under the cigar-shaped balloon is swung an aeroplane chassis equipped with powerful motors and steering apparatus, together with a light gun.

THE GREATEST SHIPYARD IN THE WORLD

View of Hog Island shipyard near Philadelphia, showing the forest of derricks rising from its fifty shipways. At the time the war ended, 35,000 persons were at work and 180 ships were in course of completion.

THE LARGEST SHIP IN THE WORLD AS A U. S. TRANSPORT

Among the German ships taken over by the United States at the outbreak of the war was the "Vaterland," the largest ship ever built. She was renamed the "Leviathan" and used as a transport, carrying 12,000 American soldiers past the submarines on each trip. She is shown here entering a French harbor at the end of a passage.

spies, and set criminal intrigues everywhere afoot against our national unity of counsel, our peace within and without, our industries and our commerce. Indeed it is now evident that its spies were here even before the war began; and it is unhappily not a matter of conjecture, but a fact proved in our courts of justice, that the intrigues which have more than once come perilously near to disturbing the peace and dislocating the industries of the country have been carried on at the instigation, with the support, and even under the personal direction of official agents of the Imperial Government accredited to the Government of the United States."

THE MASTER PLOTTER

Austria co-operated with Germany in a feeble way in these plots and propaganda, but the master plotter was Count Johann von Bernstorff, Germany's Ambassador. The Austro-Hungarian Ambassador, Constantin Theodor Dumba, Captain Franz von Papen, Captain Karl Boy-ed, Dr. Heinrich F. Albert, and Wolf von Igel, all of whom were attached to the German embassy, were associates in the intrigues. Franz von Rintelen operated independently and received his funds and instructions directly from Berlin.

One of the earliest methods of creating disorder in American munition plants and other industrial establishments engaged in war work was through labor disturbances. With that end in view a general German employment bureau was established in August, 1915, in New York City. It had branches in Philadelphia, Bridgeport, Pittsburgh, Cleveland, Chicago and Cincinnati. These cities at that time were the centers of industries engaged in furnishing munitions and war supplies to the Entente allies. Concerning this enterprise Ambassador Dumba writing to Baron Burian, Foreign Minister of Austria-Hungary, said:

A private German employment office has been established which provides employment for persons who have voluntarily given up their places, and it is already working well. We shall also join in and the widest support is assured us.

The duties of men sent from the German employment offices into munition plants may be gathered from the following frank

CHAPTER XVI

Sinking of the Lusitania

THE United States was brought face to face with the Great War and with what it meant in ruthless destruction of life when, on May 7, 1915, the crack Cunard Liner Lusitania, bound from New York to Liverpool, with 1,959 persons aboard, was torpedoed and sunk by a German submarine off Old Head of Kinsale, Southwestern Ireland. Two torpedoes reached their mark. The total number of lives lost when the ship sunk was 1,198. Of these 755 were passengers and the remainder were members of the crew. Of the drowned passengers, 124 were Americans and 35 were infants.

"Remember the Lusitania!" later became a battlecry just as "Remember the Maine!" acted as a spur to Americans during the war with Spain. It was first used by the famous "Black Watch" and later American troops shouted it as they went into battle.

The sinking of the Lusitania, with its attendant destruction of life, sent a thrill of horror through the neutral peoples of the world. General opposition to the use of submarines in attacking peaceful shipping, especially passenger vessels, crystallized as the result of the tragedy, and a critical diplomatic controversy between the United States and Germany developed. The American Government signified its determination to break off friendly relations with the German Empire unless the ruthless practices of the submarine commanders were terminated. Germany temporarily agreed to discontinue these practices.

Among the victims of the Cunarder's destruction were some of the best known personages of the Western Hemisphere. Alfred Gwynne Vanderbilt, multimillionaire; Charles Frohman, noted theatrical manager; Charles Klein, dramatist, who wrote "The Lion and the Mouse;" Justus Miles Forman, author, and Elbert Hubbard, known as Fra Elbertus, widely read iconoclastic writer, were drowned.

The ocean off the pleasant southern coast of Ireland was dotted with bodies for days after the sinking of the liner. The remains of many of the victims, however, never were recovered.

When the Lusitania prepared to sail from New York on her last trip, fifty anonymous telegrams addressed to prominent persons aboard the vessel warned the recipients not to sail with the liner. In addition to these warnings was an advertisement inserted in the leading metropolitan newspapers by the German embassy, advising neutral persons that British steamships were in danger of destruction in the war zone about the British Isles. This notice appeared the day the Lusitania sailed, May 1st, and was placed next the advertisement of the Cunard Line. Following is the advertisement:

NOTICE!

Travelers intending to embark on the Atlantic voyage are reminded that a state of war exists between Germany and her allies and Great Britain and her allies; that the zone of war includes the waters adjacent to the British Isles; that, in accordance with formal notice given by the Imperial German Government, vessels flying the flag of Great Britain, or of any of her allies, are liable to destruction in those waters and that travelers sailing in the war zone on ships of Great Britain or her allies do so at their own risk.

Imperial German Embassy
Washington, D. C., April 22, 1915.

Little or no attention was paid to the warnings, only the usual number of persons canceling their reservations. The general agent of the Cunard Line at New York assured the passengers that the Lusitania's voyage would be attended by no risk whatever, referring to the liner's speed and water-tight compartments.

THE GREAT LINER TORPEDOED

As the great Cunarder drew near the scene of her disaster, traveling at moderate speed along her accustomed route, there was news of freight steamers falling victims to Germany's undersea campaign. It was not definitely established, however, whether the liner was warned of danger.

At two o'clock on the fine afternoon of May 7th, some ten miles off the Old Head of Kinsale, the Lusitania was sighted by a submarine 1,000 yards away. A second later the track of a torpedo, soon followed by another, was seen and each missile crashed into the Lusitania's hull with rending detonations.

Many were killed or injured immediately by the explosions. Before the liner's headway was lost, some boats were lowered, and capsized as a result. The immediate listing of the steamship added to the difficulties of rescue and increased the tragical toll of dead.

Much heroism and calmness were displayed by many in the few minutes the liner remained afloat. The bearing of Frohman, Vanderbilt, Hubbard and other Americans was declared to have been particularly inspiring.

Rescue ships and naval vessels rushed to the aid of the survivors from all nearby ports of Ireland.

It has been said that the sinking of the Lusitania was carefully planned by the chiefs of the German admiralty. They expected, it was believed, to demoralize British shipping and strike terror into the minds of the British people by showing that the largest and swiftest of liners could easily be destroyed by submarines.

According to the Paris paper, *La Guerre Sociale*, published by Gustave Herve, the submarine responsible was the U-21, commanded by Lieutenant Hersing. Hersing was said to have been decorated for his deed. The U-21 afterwards was destroyed and the story of its participation in the sinking of the great Cunarder never was confirmed.

Immediately upon the news of the Lusitania disaster, President Wilson took steps to hold Germany to that "strict accountability" of which he had notified Berlin when the war-zone operations were begun earlier in the year. His first communication, protesting against the sinking of the liner in the name of humanity and demanding disavowal, indemnity and assurance that the crime would not be repeated, was despatched on May 13th. On May 30th the German reply argued that the liner carried munitions of war and probably was armed.

The following official German version of the incident by the German Admiralty Staff over the signature of Admiral Behncke was given:

"The submarine sighted the steamer, which showed no flag, May 7th, at 2.20 o'clock, Central European time, afternoon, on the southeast coast of Ireland, in fine, clear weather.

"At 3.10 o'clock one torpedo was fired at the Lusitania, which hit her starboard side below the captain's bridge. The detonation of the torpedo was followed immediately by a further explosion of extremely strong effect. The ship quickly listed to starboard and began to sink.

"The second explosion must be traced back to the ignition of quantities of ammunition inside the ship."

These extenuations were all rejected by the United States, and the next note prepared by President Wilson was of such character that Secretary of State Bryan resigned. This second communication was sent on June 11th, and on June 22d another was cabled. September 1st Germany accepted the contentions of the United States in regard to submarine warfare upon peaceful shipping. There were continued negotiations concerning the specific settlement to be made in the case of the Lusitania.

On February 4th, 1915, arrived a German proposition which, coupled with personal parleys carried on between German Ambassador von Bernstorff and United States Secretary of State Lansing, seemed in a fair way to conclude the whole controversy. It was announced on February 8th that the two nations were in substantial accord and Germany was declared to have admitted the sinking of the liner was wrong and unjustified and promised that reparation would be made.

However, a week later, when Germany took advantage of tentative American proposals concerning the disarming of merchant ships, by announcing that all armed hostile merchantmen would be treated as warships and attacked without warning, the almost completed agreement was overthrown. The renewed negotiations were continuing when the torpedoing of the cross-channel passenger ship Sussex, without warning, on March 24th, impelled the United States to issue a virtual ultimatum, demanding that the Germans immediately cease their present methods of naval warfare on pain of the rupture of diplomatic relations with the most powerful existing neutral nation.

The Lusitania, previous to her sinking, had figured in the war news, first at the conflict, when it was feared she had been captured by a German cruiser while she was dashing across the Atlantic toward Liverpool, and again in February of 1915, when she flew the American flag as a ruse to deceive submarines while

CHAPTER XVII

ITALY DECLARES WAR ON AUSTRIA

FOR many years before the great war began the great powers of Europe were divided into two great alliances, the Triple Entente, composed of Russia, France and England, and the Triple Alliance, composed of Germany, Austria and Italy. When the war began Italy refused to join with Germany and Austria. Why? The answer to this question throws a vivid light on the origin of the war.

Italy was a member of the Triple Alliance; she knew the facts, not only what was given to the public, but the inside facts. According to the terms of the alliance each member was bound to stand by each other only in case of attack. Italy refused to join with Austria and Germany because they were the aggressors. The constant assertions of the German statesmen, and of the Kaiser himself, that war had been forced upon them were declared untrue by their associate Italy in the very beginning, and the verdict of Italy was the verdict of the world. Not much was said in the beginning about Italy's abstention from war. The Germans, indeed, sneered a little and hinted that some day Italy would be made to regret her course, but now that the Teuton snake is scotched the importance of Italy's action has been perceived and appraised at its true value.

The Germans from the very beginning understood the real danger that might come to the Central Powers through Italian action. Every effort was made by the foreign office to keep her neutral. First threats were used, later promises were held out of addition to Italian territory if she would send her troops to Germany's assistance. When this failed the most strenuous efforts were made to keep Italy neutral, and a former German premier, Prince von Bülow, was sent to Italy for this purpose. Socialist leaders, too, were sent from Germany to urge the Italian Socialists to insist upon neutrality.

In July, 1914, the Italian Government was not taken by

surprise.   They had observed the increase year by year of the
German army and of the German fleet.   At the end of the Balkan
wars they had been asked whether they would agree to an Austrian
attack upon Serbia.   They had consequently long been deliberating
as to what their course should be in case of war, and they had made
up their minds that under no circumstances would they aid Germany against England.

THE MIXTURE OF RACES THAT FORMED AUSTRIA-HUNGARY

Quite independently of her long-standing friendship with
England it would be suicide to Italy in her geographical position to
enter into a war which should permit her coast to be attacked by
the English and French navies, and her participation in the Triple
Alliance always carried the proviso that it did not bind her to
fight England.   This was well known in the German foreign office,
and, indeed, in France where the writers upon war were reckoning
confidently on the withdrawing of Italy from the Triple Alliance,
and planning to use the entire forces of France against Germany.

ORIGIN OF THE TRIPLE ALLIANCE

A better understanding of the Italian position will result from
a consideration of the origin of the Triple Alliance.

CHAPTER XVIII

GLORIOUS GALLIPOLI

ON NOVEMBER 5, 1914, Great Britain declared war upon Turkey. Hostilities, however, had preceded the declaration. On November 3d the combined French and British squadrons had bombarded the entrance forts. This was merely intended to draw the fire of the forts and make an estimate of their power. From that time on a blockade was maintained, and on the 13th of December a submarine, commanded by Lieutenant Holbrook, entered the straits and torpedoed the Turkish warship Messoudieh, which was guarding the mine fields. By the end of January the blockading fleet, through constant reinforcement, had become very strong, and had seized the Island of Tenedos and taken possession of Lemnos, which nominally belonged to Greece, as bases for naval operations. On the 19th of February began the great attack upon the forts at the entrance to the Dardanelles which attracted the attention of the world for nearly a year. In order to understand the object of the Allied attack upon the Dardanelles, some description of the place may be necessary.

In Gibbon's Decline and Fall of the Roman Empire, the great historian says: "The geographers who, with the most skilful accuracy, have surveyed the form and extent of the Hellespont, assigned about sixty miles for the winding course, and about three miles for the ordinary breadth of these celebrated straits. But the narrowest part of the channel is found to the northward of the old Turkish castles between the cities of Sestus and Abydos. It was here that the adventurous Leander braved the passage of the flood for the possession of his mistress; it was here, likewise, in a place where the distance between the opposite banks cannot exceed five hundred paces, that Xerxes imposed his stupendous bridge of boats, for the purpose of transporting into Europe a hundred and seventy myriads of barbarians. A sea contracted within such narrow limits may seem but ill to deserve the epithet of broad which Homer, as well as Orpheus, has frequently bestowed

THE WORLD WAR FROM BEGINNING TO END

The Illustrations in this prospectus present a kaleidoscopic view of some of the great battles and incidents of the World War. They will give some idea of how the marvelous story of this, the greatest war in history, is illustrated in the complete book. Great battles, splendid deeds of heroism, and magnificent achievements are pictured vividly and accurately. The same care has been taken in selecting the illustrations for the book, and in writing the descriptions of them, as was used by the authors in preparing the text. The illustrations have largely been secured from official sources, the photographs having been taken under the direction of the American, British, Canadian, French and Italian governments. The authorship of the book is a guarantee to the reader that it is authentic and reliable in every detail.

GREAT PERSONAGES AND GERMAN ATROCITIES

The thoroughness that has been employed in illustrating the work with the portraits of the great personages of the war. Note the description under the illustration "Kaiser Wilhelm II of Germany." This illustration represents the German Emperor in the height of his power and as he might have continued to be except for his terrible transgression. The following illustration represents him as he is to day, despised by the world. Never has anyone except the arch-fiend himself, fallen further. In the second section of these illustrations there is shown a remarkable picture of the German Staff at the beginning of the war, which contains the portraits of all the enemy leaders who have been obliged to submit to defeat. They were responsible for the many atrocities practiced by the German nation, some of which are represented in the illustrations that follow.

INSTRUMENTS OF WAR

In the illustrations our aim has been to show how thoroughly the work pictures the Naval History of the World War, especially the great naval battles fought by the ships and sailors of Great Britain, through which the supremacy of the seas was maintained. They also portray the remarkable feat of America in transporting more than two million troops across the wide expanse of ocean. Many other important incidents of naval significance are shown. War in the air and under the water is also represented, as well as many other instruments and methods employed in modern warfare.

NOTE. The complete book contains many additional illustrations, portraits, and maps, which will not be found in this prospectus. The illustrations in the prospectus have been selected as representing the different phases of the war and will, therefore, give some idea of the more than two hundred illustrations, portraits, maps, etc., that will be found in the complete book. The illustrations, in themselves, form a Pictorial History of the War. The titles of the pictures should be read with care as they greatly aid in understanding the story told by the illustrations.

KAISER WILLIAM II OF GERMANY

Posterity will regard him as more responsible than any other human being for the sacrifice of millions of lives in the great war, as a ruler who might have been beneficent and wise, but attempted to destroy the liberties of mankind and to raise on their ruins an odious despotism. To forgive him and to forget his terrible transgressions would be to condone them.

FRANCIS JOSEPH I OF AUSTRIA, THE "OLD EMPEROR," ON A STATE OCCASION

Francis Joseph died before the war had settled the fate of the Hapsburgs. The end came on November 21, 1916, in the sixty-eighth year of his reign. His life was tragic. He lived to see his brother executed, his Queen assassinated, and his only son a suicide, with always before him the spectre of the disintegration of his many-raced empire.

SERBS DEFENDING THE MOUNTAIN PASSES LEADING TO THEIR CAPITAL

Little Serbia, before she was overwhelmed by the concentrated forces of a mighty Teuton drive, and afterward, did some fighting that astonished the world. The photo shows some of her artillery engaged in holding back the enemy in the mountain regions near Nish.

A SCENE FROM EARLY TRENCH WARFARE

From the woods in the background the British charge on an angle of the German breastworks under cover of artillery and machine-gun fire. This illustrates the early trench warfare before the development of the elaborate concrete-protected structures the Germans later devised. They can be seen wearing the famous spiked helmets which were later replaced by steel ones.

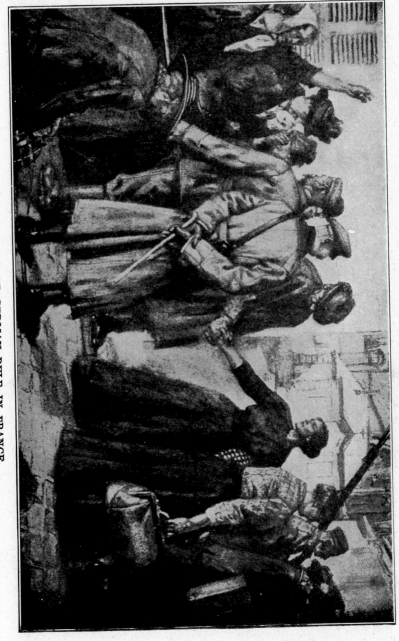

THE HORRORS OF GERMAN RULE IN FRANCE

Forcibly removing French civilians from Lille to German labor colonies. Families were ruthlessly separated and led away into slavery often worse than death.

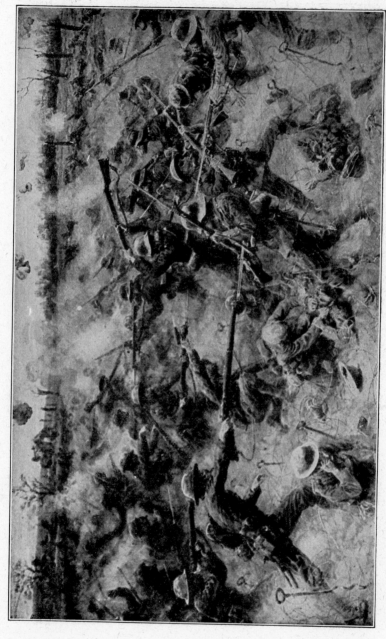

A FIGHT IN A CLOUD OF GAS

The Germans had sent over gas and in this spot it lingered. Then the infantry advanced and here, amid the British wire entanglements, the foes meet. Both sides in gas masks, they struggle amid the poisonous vapor, and when the bayonet fails they fight, like the pair in the foreground, to bring death by tearing away their opponent's mask.

ADMIRAL WILLIAM S. SIMS

Commander-in-Chief of the United States Navy in European waters.

ADMIRAL SIR DAVID BEATTY

Commander-in-Chief of the British Grand Fleet.

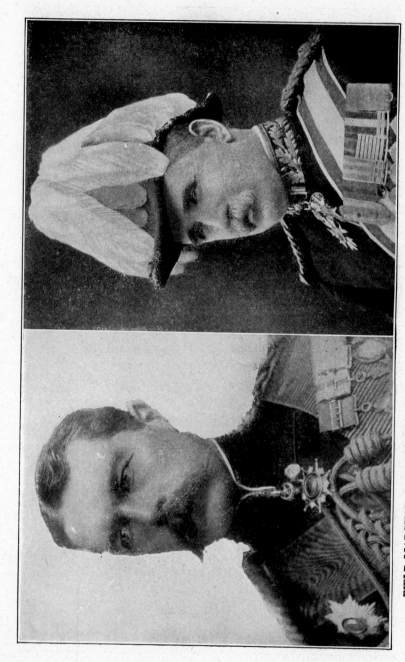

FIELD-MARSHAL EARL KITCHENER
British Secretary for War, who built up the British
army at the beginning of the war.

[FIELD-MARSHAL SIR JOHN D. FRENCH
Commander-in-chief of the British forces in France
and Belgium from the beginning of the war to December,
1915.

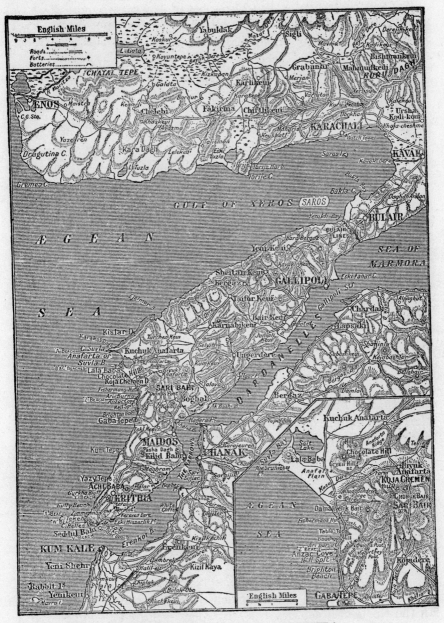

MAP OF THE GALLIPOLI PENINSULA
Showing the various landing places, with inset of the Sari-Bair Region.

upon the Hellespont. But our ideas of greatness are of a relative nature. The traveler, and especially the poet, who sailed along the Hellespont, who pursued the windings of the stream and contemplated the rural scenery which appeared on every side to terminate the prospect, insensibly lost the remembrance of the sea, and his fancy painted those celebrated straits with all the attributes of a mighty river flowing with a swift current in the midst of a woody and inland country, and, at length, through a wide mouth discharging itself into the Ægean or archipelago. Ancient Troy, seated on an eminence at the foot of Mount Ida, overlooked the mouth of the Hellespont, which scarcely received an accession of waters from the tribute of those immortal rivulets Simois and Scamander. The Grecian camp had stretched twelve miles along the shore from the Sigaean to the Rhoetian promontory, and the flanks of the army were guarded by the bravest chiefs who fought under the banner of Agamemnon. The first of those promontories was occupied by Achilles, with his invincible myrmidons, and dauntless Ajax pitched his tents on the other. After Ajax had fallen, a sacrifice to his disappointed pride and to the ingratitude of the Greeks, his sepulcher was erected on the ground where he had defended the navy against the rage of Jove and Hector, and the citizens of the rising town of Rhoetium celebrated his memory with divine honors. Before Constantine gave a just reference to the situation of Byzantium he had conceived the design of erecting the seat of empire on this celebrated spot from whence the Romans derived their fabulous origin. The extensive plain which lies below ancient Troy towards the Rhoetium promontory, and the tomb of Ajax, was first chosen for his new capital, and though the undertaking was soon relinquished, the stately remains of unfinished walls and towers attracted the notice of all who sailed through the straits of the Hellespont."

A PRIZE FOR WHICH THE NATIONS STROVE

The city of Constantinople, formerly called Byzantium, has always been a great prize for which the nations have been striving. In the thirteenth century the Crusaders captured it and placed a Flemish count on the throne; in 1358 the Turks made it the base for their inroads into Europe. From the time that Russia became a great power she had striven to secure its possession; not only thus

CHAPTER XIX

The Greatest Naval Battle in History

GERMANY'S ambition for conquest at sea had been nursed and carefully fostered for twenty years. During the decade immediately preceding the declaration of war, it had embarked upon a policy of naval upbuilding that brought it into direct conflict with England's sea policy. Thereafter it became a race in naval construction, England piling up a huge debt in its determination to construct two tons of naval shipping to every one ton built by Germany.

Notwithstanding Great Britain's efforts in this direction, Germany's naval experts, with the ruthless von Tirpitz at their head, maintained that, given a fair seaway with ideal weather conditions favoring the low visibility tactics of the German sea command, a victory for the Teutonic ships would follow. It was this belief that drew the ships of the German cruiser squadron and High Seas Fleet off the coast of Jutland and Horn Reef into the great battle that decided the supremacy of the sea.

The 31st of May, 1916, will go down in history as the date of this titanic conflict. The British light cruiser Galatea on patrol duty near Horn Reef reported at 2.20 o'clock on the afternoon of that day, that it had sighted smoke plumes denoting the advance of enemy vessels from the direction of Helgoland Bight. Fifteen minutes later the smoke plumes were in such number and volume that the advance of a considerable force to the northward and eastward was indicated. It was reasoned by Vice-Admiral Beatty, to whom the Galatea had sent the news by radio, that the enemy in rounding Horn Reef would inevitably be brought into action. The first ships of the enemy were sighted at 3.31 o'clock. These were the battle screen of fast light cruisers. Back of these were five modern battle cruisers of the highest power and armament.

The report of the battle, by an eye-witness, that was issued upon semiofficial authority of the British Government, follows:

First Phase, 3.30 P. M. May 31st. Beatty's battle cruisers,

261

consisting of the Lion, Princess Royal, Queen Mary, Tiger, Inflexible, Indomitable, Invincible, Indefatigable, and New Zealand, were on a southeasterly course, followed at about two miles distance by the four battleships of the class known as Queen Elizabeths.

Enemy light cruisers were sighted and shortly afterward the head of the German battle cruiser squadron, consisting of the new cruiser Hindenburg, the Seydlitz, Derfflinger, Lützow, Moltke, and possibly the Salamis.

Beatty at once began firing at a range of about 20,000 yards (twelve miles) which shortened to 16,000 yards (nine miles) as the fleets closed. The Germans could see the British distinctly outlined against the light yellow sky. The Germans, covered by a haze, could be very indistinctly made out by the British gunners.

The Queen Elizabeths opened fire on one after another as they came within range. The German battle cruisers turned to port and drew away to about 20,000 yards.

THE GERMAN HIGH SEAS FLEET APPEARS

Second Phase, 4.40 P. M. A destroyer screen then appeared beyond the German battle cruisers. The whole German High Seas Fleet could be seen approaching on the northeastern horizon in three divisions, coming to the support of their battle cruisers.

The German battle cruisers now turned right round 16 points and took station in front of the battleships of the High Fleet.

Beatty, with his battle cruisers and supporting battleships, therefore, had before him the whole of the German battle fleet, and Jellicoe was still some distance away.

The opposing fleets were now moving parallel to one another in opposite directions, and but for a master maneuver on the part of Beatty the British advance ships would have been cut off from Jellicoe's Grand Fleet. In order to avoid this and at the same time prepare the way so that Jellicoe might envelop his adversary, Beatty immediately also turned right around 16 points, so as to bring his ships parallel to the German battle cruisers and facing the same direction.

As soon as he was around he increased to full speed to get ahead of the Germans and take up a tactical position in advance of their line. He was able to do this owing to the superior speed of our battle cruisers.

Just before the turning point was reached, the Indefatigable

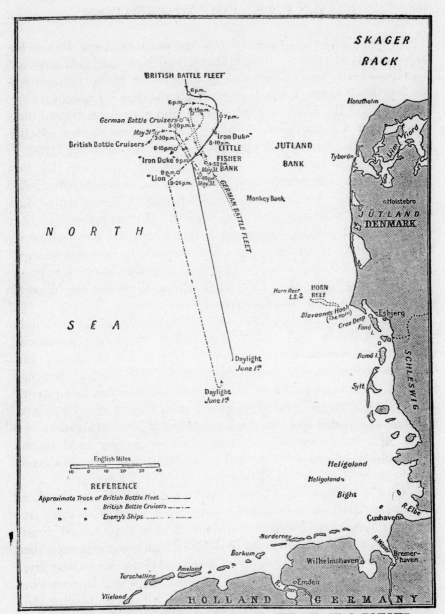

HOW THE GREAT NAVAL BATTLE OF JUTLAND WAS FOUGHT

This chart must be taken only as a general indication of the courses of the opposing fleets. Sir David Beatty, with two squadrons of battle-cruisers and one squadron of fast battleships, first steamed southward and southeastward of the German Battle-Cruiser Squadron; then, sighting the German Battle Fleet, turned northward, afterwards bearing eastward and connecting with Sir John Jellicoe's Battle Squadrons.

sank, and the Queen Mary and the Invincible also were lost at the turning point, where, of course, the High Seas Fleet concentrated their fire.

A little earlier, as the German battle cruisers were turning, the Queen Elizabeths had in similar manner concentrated their fire on the turning point and destroyed a new German battle cruiser, believed to be the Hindenburg.

Beatty had now got around and headed away with the loss of three ships, racing parallel to the German battle cruisers. The Queen Elizabeths followed behind engaging the main High Seas Fleet.

THE WARSPITE FIGHTS SIX OF THE ENEMY

Third Phase, 5 P. M. The Queen Elizabeths now turned short to port 16 points in order to follow Beatty. The Warspite jammed her steering gear, failed to get around, and drew the fire of six of the enemy, who closed in upon her.

The Germans claimed her as a loss, since on paper she ought to have been lost, but, as a matter of fact, though repeatedly straddled by shell fire with the water boiling up all around her, she was not seriously hit, and was able to sink one of her opponents. Her captain recovered control of the vessel, brought her around, and followed her consorts.

In the meantime the Barham, Valiant and Malaya turned short so as to avoid the danger spot where the Queen Mary and the Invincible had been lost, and for an hour, until Jellicoe arrived, fought a delaying action against the High Seas Fleet.

The Warspite joined them at about 5.15 o'clock, and all four ships were so successfully maneuvered in order to upset the spotting corrections of their opponents that no hits of a seriously disabling character were suffered. They had the speed over their opponents by fully four knots, and were able to draw away from part of the long line of German battleships, which almost filled up the horizon.

At this time the Queen Elizabeths were steadily firing on at the flashes of German guns at a range which varied between 12,000 and 15,000 yards, especially against those ships which were nearest them. The Germans were enveloped in a mist and only smoke and flashes were visible.

By 5.45 half of the High Seas Fleet had been left out of range, and the Queen Elizabeths were steaming fast to join hands with Jellicoe.

To return to Beatty's battle cruisers. They had succeeded in outflanking the German battle cruisers, which were, therefore, obliged to turn a full right angle to starboard to avoid being headed.

Heavy fighting was renewed between the opposing battle cruiser squadrons, during which the Derfflinger was sunk; but toward 6 o'clock the German fire slackened very considerably,

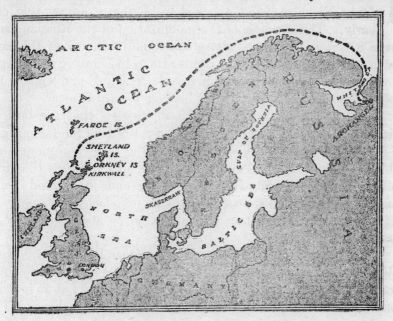

WHERE EARL KITCHENER MET HIS DEATH

showing that Beatty's battle cruisers and the Queen Elizabeths had inflicted serious damage to their immediate opponents.

THE BRITISH GRAND FLEET IN ACTION

Fourth Phase, 6 P. M. The Grand Fleet was now in sight, and, coming up fast in three directions, the Queen Elizabeths altered their course four points to the starboard and drew in toward the enemy to allow Jellicoe room to deploy into line.

The Grand Fleet was perfectly maneuvered and the very difficult operation of deploying between the battle cruisers and the Queen Elizabeths was perfectly timed.

CHAPTER XX

THE RUSSIAN CAMPAIGN

IN THE very beginning Russia had marked out one point for attack. This was the city of Cracow. No doubt the Grand Duke Nicholas had not hoped to be able to invest that city early. The slowness of the mobilization of the Russian army made a certain prudence advisable at the beginning of the campaign. But the great success of his armies in Lemberg encouraged more daring aims. He had invested Przemysl, and Galicia lay before him. Accordingly, he set his face toward Cracow.

Cracow, from a military point of view, is the gate both of Vienna and Berlin. A hundred miles west of it is the famous gap of Moravia, between the Carpathian and the Bohemian mountains, which leads down into Austria. Through this gap runs the great railway connecting Silesia with Vienna, and the Grand Duke knew that if he could capture Cracow he would have an easy road before him to the Austrian capital. Cracow also is the key of Germany.

Seventy miles from the city lies the Oder River. Any army might enter Germany by this gate and turn the line of Germany's frontier fortresses. The Oder had been well fortified, but an invader coming from Cracow might move upon the western bank. The Russian plan no doubt was to threaten both enemy capitals. Moreover, an advance of Russia from Cracow would take its armies into Silesia, full of coal and iron mines, and one of the greatest manufacturing districts in the German Empire. This would be a real success, and all Germany would feel the blow.

Another reason for the Russian advance in Galicia was her desire to control the Galician oil wells. To Germany petrol had become one of the foremost munitions of war. Since she could not obtain it from either America or Russia she must get it from Austria, and the Austrian oil fields were all in Galicia. This, in itself, would explain the Galician campaign. Moreover, through the Carpathian Mountains it was possible to make frequent raids

273

THE FAMOUS WITHERED ARM

A most unusual photograph of the ex-Kaiser showing his withered left arm. The sale of this picture was forbidden in Germany. The other figure is the Hetman of the Ukrainia Skoropadski.

THE FIRST STAGE HOMEWARDS
Stretcher bearers bringing in wounded from the battlefield to the
collecting posts.

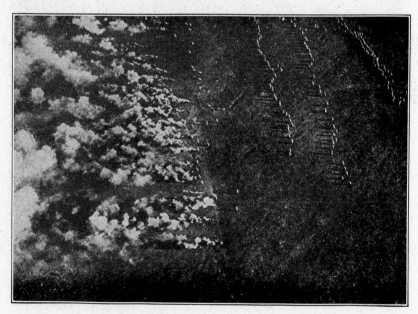

GERMAN FRIGHTFULNESS FROM THE AIR
A gas attack on the eastern front photographed by a Russian airman.

AN OBSERVATION POST
Watching the effect of gun fire from a sand-bagged ruin near the German lines.

KING ALBERT AT THE HEAD OF THE HEROIC SOLDIERS OF BELGIUM

It is universally agreed that the Belgian monarch was no figurehead general but a real leader of his troops. It was these men, facing annihilation, who astonished the world by opposing the German military machine successfully enough to allow France to get her armies into shape and prevent the immediate taking of Paris that was planned by Germany.

THE TERRIBLE FLANDERS MUD

A German battery endeavoring to escape from a British advance sinks in the mud and the gunners are endeavoring to pull the gun out with ropes.

King Albert I   Queen Elizabeth

THE HEROIC RULERS OF BELGIUM

© *International News Service.*

YPRES, BATTLE-TORN BUT IMPERISHABLE

The old Flemish town of Ypres, stands today a monument to the bulldog tenacity of Great Britain's troops. After they fastened on it, neither the bloody fighting of the early war nor the crucial great offensives of the later days could shake their grip   The famous medieval Cloth Hall is shown at the right of the picture in ruins.

Photos from International Film Service.

THE GERMAN CHANCELLORS

On the right is Theobald von Bethmann-Hollweg who is held responsible in large measure for bringing on the war. On the left is Prince Maximilian of Baden, the Kaiser's camouflage chancellor who was appointed in a vain attempt to fool the American people into thinking that a democratic government had been set up in Germany.

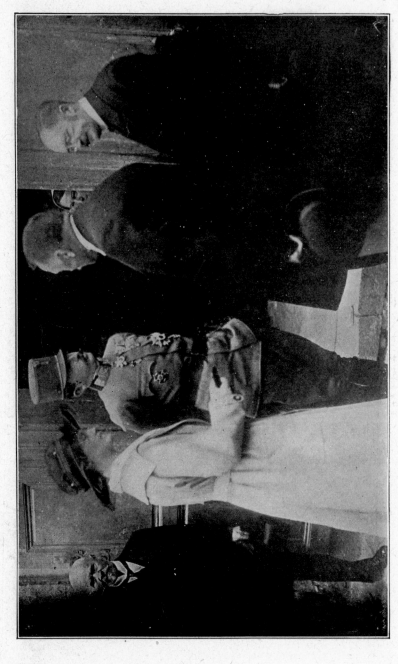

THE DEPOSED RULERS OF AUSTRIA-HUNGARY

The ex-Emperor Charles and his wife, the ex-Empress Zita, in deep conversation with Hungarian leaders who are explaining the distressing situation confronting the country.

into Hungary, and Russia understood well the feeling of Hungary toward her German allies. She hoped that when Hungary perceived her regiments sacrificed and her plains overrun by Russian troops, she would regret that she had allowed herself to be sacrificed to Prussian ambition. The Russians, therefore, suddenly moved toward Cracow.

Then von Hindenburg came to the rescue. The supreme command of the Austrian forces was given to him. The defenses of Cracow were strengthened under the direction of the Germans, and a German army advanced from the Posen frontier toward the northern bank of the Vistula. The advance threatened the Russian right, and, accordingly, within ten days' march of Cracow, the Russians stopped. The German offensive in Poland had begun. The news of the German advance came about the fifth of October. Von Hindenburg, who had been fighting in East Prussia, had at last perceived that nothing could be gained there. The vulnerable part of Russia was the city of Warsaw. This was the capital of Poland, with a population of about three-quarters of a million. If he could take Warsaw, he would not only have pleasant quarters for the winter but Russia would be so badly injured that no further offensive from her need be anticipated for a long period. Von Hindenburg had with him a large army. In this center he probably had three-quarters of a million men, and on his right the Austrian army in Cracow, which must have reached a million.

TWO MILLIONS AGAINST TWO AND A HALF MILLIONS

Counting the troops operating in East Prussia and along the Carpathians, and the garrison of Przemysl, the Teuton army must have had two and a half million soldiers. Russia, on the other hand, though her mobilization was still continuing, at this time could not have had as many as two million men in the whole nine hundred miles of her battle front.

The Grand Duke Nicholas, divining the intentions of the German commander, determined to take no risks. If he should advance west of the Vistula he knew very well, from the geographical formation of the country and the scarcity of railroads, that he would have difficulty in bringing up supplies. He, therefore, determined to keep behind the Vistula. The Vistula River runs in a general way north by west through the Polish plain. Warsaw lies on its left; and the river, almost all of whose length in Russia is deep and unfordable, is bridged only on two points, at Warsaw and at Ivangorod. These two points, therefore, had to be protected. Very few railroad lines run from the German frontier to the river. Along these railroad lines the German armies would naturally move.

On the south Von Hindenburg planned that the Austrians should advance from Cracow, relieve Przemysl and cut off a Russian retreat behind the San. In the north there should be a movement up the Vistula, by means of the Vistula, and the Thorn Lowicz railway. The center would advance more directly upon Warsaw. He evidently planned that his right wing should cross the Vistula at the Narrows at Josefov, far in the south, where the Russians would be fighting at a point where their communications were at their worst. Once over the Vistula he would move northeast to Lublin and then to the rear of Warsaw. The Grand Duke well understood what was being planned. He took great pains to give the Germans false information, and misled them into believing that he did not mean to defend Warsaw.

On the 10th of October von Hindenburg's center was at Lodz, his left and right moving rapidly according to the plan outlined. The Russians in Galicia had retreated fast, making one desperate effort to capture Przemysl before they left, an attempt that was unsuccessful. The German advance was slow and deliberate. As they moved they built good roads so as to bring up supplies, and also provide an easy method of retreat. German dirigibles and airplanes were sent above the city of Warsaw, some of them dropping bombs and others showers of leaflets, directed to the Poles, the Catholics and the soldiers, and aiming to produce disorder.

THE BATTLE BEFORE WARSAW

The fight for Warsaw began on Friday the 16th and continued for three days, von Hindenburg being personally in command. The Grand Duke depended mainly on the Siberian corps, and was aided by batteries of heavy guns served by Japanese gunners. Of the Russian army an English correspondent has this to say: "It is stimulating to see the Russian soldier in his habits as he lives and fights. I have seen many thousands of them camped in the rain, swamped in bogs or marching indefatigably over the

THE GERMAN ATTACK ON THE ROAD TO PETROGRAD

roads, which are long quagmires of mud, always with an air of stolid contentment, and the look of being bent on business. They include Baltic Province men speaking German. Jews from Riga and Libau are brigaded with huge Siberians whose marching must constitute a world record. The Cossacks are past counting, and with them are long-coated, tight-belted Circassians and Kalmucks, all representing a mixture of races and languages like that of the British Empire itself. This is an army in which every man has fought. Most of them have been in hand-to-hand conflict with the Germans. It is impossible not to admire these endless battalions of Siberians; they are common objects of this countryside. I came past Suwalki as they were moving up column after column in gray overcoats, a swing in the rhythm of their stride, like the kilts of Highlanders. It was they who bore the brunt of the fighting, unsupported by artillery, in the forests of Augustovo. These are the men who marched forty miles, starting at midnight, and then went into action, and delivered a bayonet charge which their officers still boast about today. The cloud of patrols, mostly Cossacks, which flits unceasingly along the German front, is the subject of innumerable stories. When the news was issued that the Kaiser had come east to take command of his army on this front, a Cossack came in, driving before him a plump, distressed Prussian captain, whom he had gleaned during a day's work. 'I've brought him,' he announced. 'I knew him by his mustache,' and he produced an old picture postcard from his breast, showing the Kaiser." The battle before Warsaw at first seemed even, but on Monday the Germans found themselves in trouble. A Russian attack on their left wing had come with crushing force. Von Hindenburg found his left wing thrown back, and the whole German movement thrown into disorder. Meanwhile the attempt to cross the Vistula at Josefov had also been a failure. The Russians allowed the Germans to pass with slight resistance, waited until they arrived at the village Kazimirjev, a district of low hills and swampy flats, and then suddenly overwhelmed them.

THE GERMANS IN FULL RETREAT

Next day the Russians crossed the river themselves, and advanced along the whole line, driving the enemy before them, through great woods of spruce out into the plains on the west.

CHAPTER XXI

Bulgaria Joins Germany

FOR more than half a century the Balkans have presented a problem which has disturbed the minds of the statesmen of Europe. Again and again, during that period, it has seemed that in the Balkan mountains might be kindled a blaze which might set the world afire. Balkan politics is a labyrinth in which one might easily be lost. The inhabitants of the Balkans represent many races, each with its own ambition, and, for the most part, military. There were Serbs, and Bulgarians, and Turks, and Roumanians, and Greeks, and their territorial divisions did not correspond to their nationalities. The land was largely mountainous, with great gaps that make it, in a sense, the highway of the world. From 1466 to 1878 the Balkans was in the dominion of the Turks. In the early days, while the Turks were warring against Hungary, their armies marched through the Balkan hills. The natives kept apart, and preserved their language, religion and customs.

In the nineteenth century, as the Turks grew weaker, their subject people began to seek independence. Greece came first, and, in 1829, aided by France, Russia and Great Britain, she became an independent kingdom. Serbia revolted in 1804, and by 1820 was an autonomous state, though still tributary to Turkey. In 1859, Roumania became autonomous. The rising of Bulgaria in 1876, however, was really the beginning of the succession of events which ultimately led to the present Great War. The Bulgarian insurrection was crushed by the Turks in such a way as to stir the indignation of the whole world. What are known as the "Bulgarian Atrocities" seem mild today, but they led to the Russo-Turkish War in 1877.

The treaty of Berlin, by which that war was settled in 1878, was one of those treaties which could only lead to trouble. It deprived Russia of much of the benefit of her victory, and left nearly every racial question unsettled. Roumania lost Bessarabia, which was mainly inhabited by Roumanians. Bosnia and Herzegovina were handed over to the administration of Austria. Turkey was allowed to retain Macedonia, Albania and Thrace. Serbia was given Nish, but had no outlet to the sea. Greece obtained Thessaly, and a new province was made of the country south of the Balkans called Eastern Rumelia. From that time on, quarrel after quarrel made up the history of the Balkan peoples, each of whom sought the assistance and support of some one of the great powers. Russia and Austria were constantly intriguing with the new states, in the hope of extending their own domains in the direction of Constantinople.

CENTER OF INTRIGUE

The history of Bulgaria shows that that nation has been continually the center of these intrigues. In 1879 they elected as their sovereign Prince Alexander of Battenburg, whose career might almost be called romantic. A splendid soldier and an accomplished gentleman, he stands out as an interesting figure in the sordid politics of the Balkans. He identified himself with his new country. In 1885 he brought about a union with Eastern Rumelia, which led to a disagreement with Russia.

Serbia, doubtless at Russian instigation, suddenly declared war, but was overwhelmed by Prince Alexander in short order. Russia then abducted Prince Alexander, but later was forced to restore him. However, Russian intrigues, and his failure to obtain support from one of the great powers, forced his abdication in 1886.

In 1887 Prince Ferdinand of Saxe-Coburg-Gotha became the Prince of Bulgaria. He, also, was a remarkable man, but not the romantic figure of his predecessor. He seems to have been a sort of a parody of a king. He was fond of ostentation, and full of ambition. He was a personal coward, but extremely cunning. During his long reign he built up Bulgaria into a powerful, independent kingdom, and even assumed the title of Czar of Bulgaria. During the first days of his reign he was kept safely on the throne by his mother, the Princess Clementine, a daughter of Louis Phillippe, who, according to Gladstone, was the cleverest woman in Europe, and for a few years Bulgaria was at peace. In 1908 he declared Bulgaria independent, and its independence was recognized by Turkey on the payment of an indemnity. During this period Russia was the

CHAPTER XXIV

IMMORTAL VERDUN

FRANCE was revealed to herself, to Germany and to the world as the heroic defender of civilization, as a defender defying death in the victory of Verdun. There, with the gateway to Paris lying open at its back, the French army, in the longest pitched battle in all history, held like a cold blue rock against the uttermost man power and resources of the German army.

General von Falkenhayn, Chief of the German General Staff and military dictator of the Teutonic allies, there met disaster and disgrace. There the mettle of the Crown Prince was tested and he was found to be merely a thing of straw, a weak creature whose mind was under the domination of von Falkenhayn.

For the tremendous offensive which was planned to end the war by one terrific thrust, von Falkenhayn had robbed all the other fronts of effective men and munitions. Field Marshal von Hindenburg and his crafty Chief of Staff, General Ludendorf, had planned a campaign against Russia designed to put that tottering military Colossus out of the war. The plans were upon a scale that might well have proved successful. The Kaiser, influenced by the Crown Prince and by von Falkenhayn, decreed that the Russian campaign must be postponed and that von Hindenburg must send his crack troops to join the army of the Crown Prince fronting Verdun. Ludendorf promptly resigned as Chief of Staff to von Hindenburg and suggested that the Field Marshal also resign. That grim old warrior declined to take this action, preferring to remain idle in East Prussia and watch what he predicted would be a useless effort on the western front. His warning to the General Staff was explicit, but von Falkenhayn coolly ignored the message.

Why did Germany select this particular point for its grand offensive? The answer is to be found in a demend made by the great Junker associations of Germany in May, 1915, nine months

313

before the attack was undertaken.   That demand was to the effect that Verdun should be attacked and captured.   They declared that the Verdun fortifications made a menacing salient thrust into the rich iron fields of the Briey basin.   From this metalliferous field of Lorraine came the ore that supplied eighty per cent of the steel required for German and Austrian guns and munitions.   These fields of Briey were only twenty miles from the great guns of Verdun. They were French territory at the beginning of the war and had been seized by the army of the Crown Prince, co-operating with the Army of Metz because of their immense value to the Germans in war making.

As a preliminary to the battle, von Falkenhayn placed a semicircle of huge howitzers and rifles around the field of Briey. Then assembling the vast forces drained from all the fronts and having erected ammunition dumps covering many acres, the great battle commenced with a surprise attack upon the village of Haumont on February 21, 1916.

GAINING THE OUTER DEFENSES

The first victory of the Germans at that point was an easy one. The great fort of Douaumont was the next objective.   This was taken on February 25th after a concentrated bombardment that for intensity surpassed anything that heretofore had been shown in the war.

Von Falkenhayn, personally superintending the disposition of guns and men, had now penetrated the outer defenses of Verdun. The tide was running against the French, and shells, more shells for the guns of all caliber; men, more men for the earthworks surrounding the devoted city were needed.   The narrow-gauge railway connecting Verdun with the great French depots of supplies was totally inadequate for the transportation burdens suddenly cast upon it. In this desperate emergency a transport system was born of necessity, a system that saved Verdun.   It was fleet upon fleet of motor trucks, all sizes, all styles; anything that could pack a few shells or a handful of men was utilized.   The backbone of the system was a greet fleet of trucks driven by men whose average daily rest was four hours, and upon whose horizon-blue uniforms the stains of snow and sleet, of dust and mud, were indelibly fixed through the winter, spring, summer and fall of 1916, for the glori-

LEADING GERMAN GENERALS

Von Hindenburg, Chief of the German General Staff; von Ludendorff, Strategist of the General Staff; von Moltke, dismissed by the Kaiser for incompetency; von Mackensen, Commander in the East; Crown Prince Rupprecht of Bavaria, Army Commander in the West.

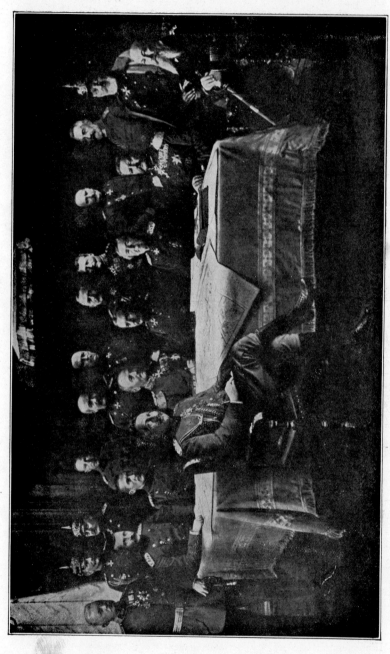

Photo by Press Illustrating Service.

THE GERMAN GENERAL STAFF

von Mackensen   von Moltke   Cr. Pr. Wilhelm   von Falkenhayn   von Beseler   von Bethmann-Hollweg
von Bülow   Duke Albrecht   Ludendorf   von Einem   von Hindenburg   von Heeringen
        Crown Prince Rupprecht   von Kluck   von Haeseler   von Tirpitz
                Kaiser Wilhelm II   von Emmich

AN AIRPLANE CONVOY
Food ships successfully convoyed by seaplanes in clear weather when submarines
were easier to detect.

BRITISH LIGHT ARTILLERY GETTING IN ON THE GALLOP

Always the guns must follow closely in the wake of the infantry to break up German counter attacks and hold the ground gained. Here a detachment of the Royal Horse Artillery storms through a deserted Flanders village, straining every nerve to save those few seconds that may mean the saving or the loss of the new positions won.

GENERAL PERSHING AND MARSHAL JOFFRE

The Commander-in-Chief of the American Expeditionary Forces chatting with the veteran Marshal of France, the hero of the first battle of the Marne.

MARSHAL FERDINAND FOCH, GENERALISSIMO OF THE ALLIED ARMIES IN THE WEST

No leader could command greater confidence than the brilliant strategist to whom was mainly due the great victory of the Marne in the first autumn of the war. He also directed the French offensive on the Somme in 1916 and in November, 1917, he was chosen as the French representative and subsequently chairman of the Central Military Committee appointed to assist the Supreme Allied War Council. Marshal Foch was formerly for five years lecturer on strategy and tactics at the Ecole de Guerre. At the close of the war he said to the Allied armies: "You have won the greatest battle in history and saved the most sacred cause—the liberty of the world."

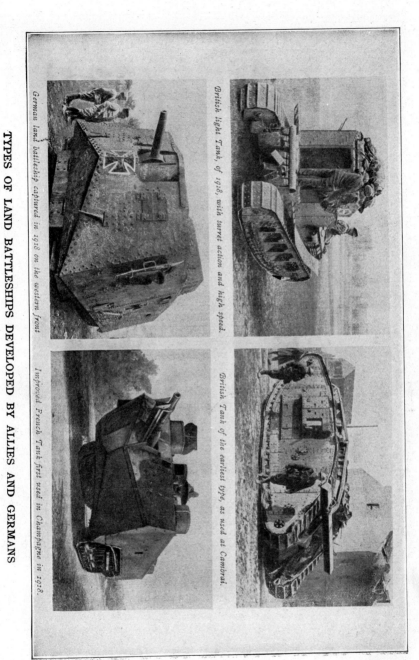

British light Tank, of 1918, with turret action and high speed.

German land battleship captured in 1918 on the western front

British Tank of the earliest type, as used at Cambrai.

Improved French Tank first used in Champagne in 1918.

TYPES OF LAND BATTLESHIPS DEVELOPED BY ALLIES AND GERMANS

CHARGING ON GERMAN TRENCHES IN GAS MASKS

Each British soldier carried two gas-proof helmets. At the first alarm of gas the helmet was instantly adjusted, for to breathe even a whiff of the yellow cloud meant death or serious injury. This picture shows the earlier type before the respirator mask was devised to keep up with Germany's development of gas warfare.

ous engagement continued from February 21st until November 2d, when the Germans were forced into full retreat from the field of honor, the evacuation of Fort Vaux putting a period to Germany's disastrous plan and to von Falkenhayn's military career.

Lord Northcliffe, describing the early days of the immortal battle, wrote:

"Verdun is, in many ways, the most extraordinary of battles. The mass of metal used on both sides is far beyond all parallel; the transformation on the Douaumont Ridge was more suddenly dramatic than even the battle of the Marne; and, above all, the duration of the conflict already looks as if it would surpass anything in history. More than a month has elapsed since, by the kindness of General Joffre and General Petain, I was able to watch the struggle from various vital viewpoints. The battle had then been raging with great intensity for a fortnight, and, as I write, four to five thousand guns are still thundering round Verdun. Impossible, therefore, any man to describe the entire battle. The most one can do is to set down one's impressions of the first phases of a terrific conflict, the end of which cannot be foreseen.

"My chief impression is one of admiration for the subtle powers of mind of the French High Command. General Joffre and General Castelnau are men with especially fine intellects tempered to terrible keenness. Always they have had to contend against superior numbers. In 1870, when they were subalterns, their country lost the advantage of its numerous population by abandoning general military service at a time when Prussia was completely realizing the idea of a nation in arms. In 1914, when they were commanders, France was inferior to a still greater degree in point of numbers to Prussianized Germany. In armament, also, France was inferior at first to her enemy. The French High Command has thus been trained by adversity to do all that human intellect can against almost overwhelming hostile material forces. General Joffre, General Castelnau—and, later, General Petain, who at a moment's notice displaced General Herr—had to display genius where the Germans were exhibiting talent, and the result is to be seen at Verdun. They there caught the enemy in a series of traps of a kind hitherto unknown in modern warfare—something elemental, and yet subtle, neo-primitive, and befitting the atavistic character of the Teuton. They caught him in a web of his own unfulfilled boasts.

"The enemy began by massing a surprising force on the western front. Tremendous energy and organizing power were the marks of his supreme efforts to obtain a decision. It was usually reckoned that the Germans maintain on all fronts a field army of about seventy-four and a half army corps, which at full strength number three million men. Yet, while holding the Russians from Riga to the south of the Pripet Marshes, and maintaining a show of force in the Balkans, Germany seems to have succeeded in bringing up nearly two millions and a half of men for her grand spring offensive in the west. At one time her forces in France and Flanders were only ninety divisions. But troops and guns were withdrawn in increasing numbers from Russia and Serbia in December, 1915, until there were, it is estimated, a hundred and eighteen divisions on the Franco-British-Belgian front. A large number of six-inch and twelve-inch Austrian howitzers were added to the enormous Krupp batteries. Then a large proportion of new recruits of the 1916 class were moved into Rhineland depots to serve as drafts for the fifty-nine army corps, and it is thought that nearly all the huge shell output that had accumulated during the winter was transported westward.

ATTACKING WITH SUCCESSIVE WAVES OF INFANTRY

"The French Staff reckoned that Verdun would be attacked when the ground had dried somewhat in the March winds. It was thought that the enemy movement would take place against the British front in some of the sectors of which there were chalk undulations, through which the rains of winter quickly drained. The Germans skilfully encouraged this idea by making an apparent preliminary attack at Lihons, on a five-mile front with rolling gas-clouds and successive waves of infantry. During this feint the veritable offensive movement softly began on Saturday, February 19, 1916, when the enormous masses of hostile artillery west, east, and north of the Verdun salient started registering on the French positions. Only in small numbers did the German guns fire, in order not to alarm their opponents. But even this trial bombardment by shifts was a terrible display of power, calling forth all the energies of the outnumbered French gunners to main-

CHAPTER XXV

CANADA'S MAGNIFICENT SACRIFICE

ABSOLUTE necessity for man power early in the war drove England and all of England's possessions to the discussion of conscription. At first volunteering was the rule throughout the empire. Sensational advertising campaigns were inaugurated, great outdoor meetings were held in every populous center, and every spur of patriotism and individual pride was resorted to for the purpose of filling the ranks of Kitchener's great armies.

As the Teutonic tide rose inundating Poland, Belgium and northern France, it was realized that nothing short of the most drastic measures would produce the man power needed to hold the Hun hordes in check. A last vivid, vigorous effort at volunteering was decided upon, and the Earl of Derby was put in charge. He was a man of iron will, one of few words, and of resolute determination. He served notice upon his countrymen that those who would not volunteer would speedily be taken by conscription. In response to his far-flung efforts, 2,800,000 men volunteered to don khaki for the empire. This was in the British Isles alone. Nowhere in history may be found a volunteering campaign that can approach this in its fiery, patriotic appeals and its magnificent results.

THE SPLENDID RESPONSE OF CANADA

Worthy to rank beside the wonderful record of the British Isles is the war effort of Canada. Conscription came to England following the Earl of Derby's campaign, but there was no conscription in Canada until comparatively late in the war. Yet between August 3, 1914, and July 1, 1918, Canada enlisted for the war a total of 552,601 men. This included 56,081 drafted men. A considerable number of Canadian volunteers came from the United States during the early days of the war, when this country was still a neutral and striving diligently to bring peace to the

323

world. Of Canada's total enrolment, 42,919 died. Of these, 27,040 were killed outright in action, 9,280 died of wounds, 2,257 died of disease, and 4,342 were returned as missing. Most of

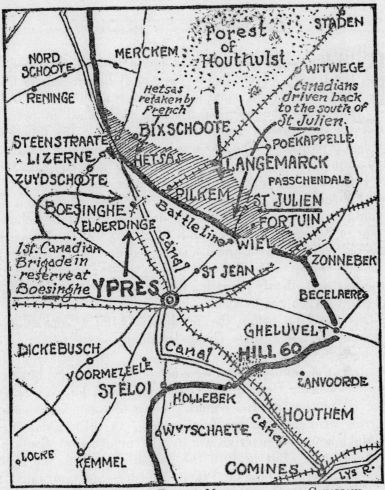

THE TOWN OF YPRES IS FULL OF MEMORIES FOR THE CANADIANS

these presumably were buried in the chalk-pitted chasms of the Somme, that most voracious of battle-fields. Canadian prisoners of war numbered, 2,274 ,and the total number of Canadian wounded during four years was 113,007.

At first there was sharp division of opinion in Canada but this speedily disappeared, as was evidenced in a speech delivered

CHAPTER XXXI

RED REVOLUTION IN RUSSIA

THE Russian Revolution was not a sudden movement of the people. Long before the war it had raised its head. The Duma itself came into existence as one of its fruits; but when the war began all parties joined in patriotic support of the Russian armies and laid aside for the time their cherished grievances. The war was immensely popular. Slavonic nationalism turned against Austria-Hungary and Germany who were bent upon crushing the Slavonic sister state, Serbia. The Liberal elements saw in Germany the stronghold of reaction and of militarism, and trusted that its downfall would be followed by that of Russian autocracy. But so glaring was the incapacity of the old régime, that a union was formed during the war by all the Liberal parties. This group united on the single aim of pushing on the war, and silently preparing for the moment when the catastrophe to Czarism was to come.

This was long before the revolution. But a conviction of the necessity of immediate change gradually came to all. The Czar himself brought matters to an issue. His vacillation, his appointment of ministers who were not only reactionary, but were suspected of being German tools, were too much for even honest supporters of the Imperial régime. Some of these reactionaries, it is true, were easily driven from power. In 1915 Sukhomlinov and Maklakov were overthrown by the influence of the army and the Duma. But in 1916 the parasites came to life again. M. Boris Stuermer became Prime Minister, and appointed as Minister of the Interior the notorious Protopopov. On November 14, 1916, Miliukov, the leader of the Constitutional Democrats, or Cadet Party, attacked the Premier in one of the fiercest speeches ever made in the Russian Duma. Stuermer was compelled to resign, but his successor, M. Trepov, though an honest man with high ambitions, was forced to retain Protopopov at the Interior. For a moment there was calm. But it was the calm before the storm.

The Russian Revolution, now recognized as the most bloody revolution in history, began with the assassination of a single man. This man was Gregory Novikh, known throughout the world under the name of Rasputin. A Siberian peasant by birth, immoral, filthy in person, untrained in mind, he had early received the nickname of Rasputin, which means "ne'er-do-well," on account of his habits. A drunkard, and a libertine always, he posed as a sort of saint and miracle worker, let his hair grow long, and tramped about the world barefoot.

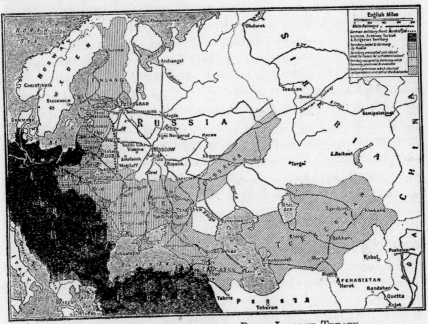

RUSSIA AS PARTITIONED BY THE BREST-LITOVSK TREATY

Rasputin had left his district of Tobolsk and at Moscow had started a new cult, where mystical séances were mingled with debauchery. Through Madame Verubova he had been introduced to the Empress herself. He became the friend of Count Witte, of Stuermer, and Protopopov was his tool. Rumor credited him with exercising an extraordinary influence upon the Czarina, and through her upon the Czar. This influence was thought to be responsible for many of the Czar's unpopular policies. In times of great public agitation the wildest rumors are easily taken for truth and the absurd legends which were easily associated with his

CHAPTER XLII

CHÂTEAU-THIERRY, FIELD OF GLORY

NOWHERE in American history may be found a more glorious record than that which crowned with laurel the American arms at Château-Thierry. Here the American Marines and divisions comprising both volunteers and selected soldiers, were thrown before the German tide of invasion like a huge khaki-colored breakwater. Germany knew that a test of its empire had come. To break the wall of American might it threw into the van of the attack the Prussian Guard backed by the most formidable troops of the German and Austrian empires. The object was to put the fear of the Hun into the hearts of the Yankees, to overwhelm them, to drive straight through them as the prow of a battleship shears through a heavy sea. If America could be defeated, Germany's way to a speedy victory was at hand. If America held—well, that way lay disaster.

And the Americans held. Not only did they hold but they counter-attacked with such bloody consequences to the German army that Marshal Foch, seizing the psychological moment for his carefully prepared counter-offensive, gave the word for a general attack.

With Château-Thierry and the Marne as a hinge, the clamp of the Allies closed upon the defeated Germans. From Switzerland to the North Sea the drive went forward, operating as huge pincers cutting like chilled steel through the Hindenburg and the Kriemhild lines. It was the beginning of autocracy's end, the end of *Der Tag* of which Germany had dreamed.

The matchless Marines and the other American troops suffered a loss that staggered America. It was a loss, however, that was well worth while. The heroic young Americans who held the might of Germany helpless and finally rolled them back defeated from the field of battle, and who paid for that victory with their lives, made certain the speedy end of the world's bloodiest war.

The story of the American army's effective operations in France

THE SINKING OF THE GERMAN CRUISER "BLUECHER"

This dramatic photograph from the great North Sea Battle in 1915 shows the stricken ship just as she turned turtle and was about to sink. Officers and men can be seen swarming like ants on the upper side of the hull. Others, who either fell or preferred to take their chance in the sea, are shown swimming away from the wreck.

GERMANY BRINGS THE WAR TO EAST COAST TOWNS OF ENGLAND

By raids with light cruisers on the coast towns, and Zeppelins and airplanes further inland, Germany sought to frighten the British populace. At Hartlepool, where this scene was enacted, several civilians, some of them women and children, were killed by bursting shells of the raiders.

From a painting by F. Gueldry to illustrate an official report.

GERMAN ATROCITIES

At Senlis, Department of Oise, on September 2, 1914. French captives were made to walk in the open so as to be hit by French bullets. Many were killed and wounded. The townsman on the left was struck in the knee. A German officer asked to see the wound and shot him through the shoulder. On the right a German officer is seen torturing a wounded French soldier by beating him in the face with a stick.

THE SUPREME EXPONENTS OF GERMAN FRIGHTFULNESS

On the left, General von Bissing, military commander of Belgium. On the right, Grand Admiral von Tirpitz, who inspired the German submarine campaign.

FAMOUS BRITISH GENERALS

General Smith-Dorrien, British Corps Commander in the famous retreat from Mons; Generals Plumer, Rawlinson and Byng, Commanders on the Western Front; General Birdwood, Commander of the Australian-New Zealand troops at Gallipoli.

FAMOUS FRENCH GENERALS

Marshal Pétain, Commander-in-Chief of the French armies in the West; Generals Mangin, Gouraud and Humbert, Army Commanders in the West; General Gallieni, Commander of Paris, who sent forward an army in taxicabs to save the day at the First Battle of the Marne.

DRIVING THE GERMAN COMMERCE RAIDERS OFF THE SEAS

The British light cruiser, "Highflyer," sinking the "Kaiser Wilhelm der Grosse" off the West Coast of Africa early in the war. The commerce-destroyer was attacking a British steamer when the cruiser came up and sent her to the bottom. Inserts show both ships.

ESCAPING A TORPEDO BY RAPID MANEUVERING

This destroyer escaped a torpedo from a hunted submarine by quick turning. Generally the torpedo travels at about fifteen feet under water.

from Cantigny to the reduction of the St. Mihiel salient, is one long record of victories. To the glory of American arms must be recorded the fact that at no time and at no place in the World War did the American forces retreat before the German hosts.

In the latter days of May, 1918, the Allied forces in France seemed near defeat. The Germans were steadily driving toward Paris. They had swept over the Chemin des Dames and the papers from day to day were chronicling wonderful successes. The Chemin des Dames had been regarded as impregnable, but the Germans passed it apparently without the slightest difficulty. They were advancing on a forty-mile front and on May 28th had reached the Aisne, with the French and British steadily falling back. The anxiety of the Allies throughout the world was indescribable. This was the great German "Victory Drive" and each day registered a new Allied defeat. Newspaper headlines were almost despairing.

THE FIRST AMERICAN OFFENSIVE

On May 29th, however, in quiet type, under great headlines announcing a German gain of ten miles in which the Germans had taken twenty-five thousand prisoners and crossed two rivers, had captured Soissons, and were threatening Rheims, there appeared in American papers a quiet little despatch from General Pershing. It read as follows:

"This morning in Picardy our troops attacked on a front of one and one-fourth miles, advanced our lines, and captured the village of Cantigny. We took two hundred prisoners, and inflicted on the enemy severe losses in killed and wounded. Our casualties were relatively small. Hostile counter-attacks broke down under our fire." This was the first American offensive.

The American troops had now been in Europe almost a year. At first but a small force, they had been greeted in Paris and in London with tremendous enthusiasm. Up to this point they had done little or nothing, but the small force which passed through Paris in the summer of 1917 had been growing steadily. By this time the American army numbered more than eight hundred thousand men. They had been getting ready; in camps far behind the lines they had been trained, not only by their own officers, but by some of the greatest experts in the French and the British armies. Thousands of officers and men who, but a few months before, had been busily engaged in civilian pursuits, had now learned something of the art of war. They had been supplied with a splendid equipment, with great guns and with all the modern requirements of an up-to-date army.

For some months, here and there, on the French and British lines, small detachments of American troops flanked on both sides by the Allied forces, had been learning the art of war. Here and there they had been under fire. At Cantigny itself they had resisted attack. On May 27th General Pershing had reported "In Picardy, after violent artillery preparations, hostile infantry detachments succeeded in penetrating our advance positions in two points. Our troops counter-attacked, completely expelling the enemy and entering his lines." They had also been fighting that day in the Waevre sector where a raiding party had been repulsed. There had been other skirmishes, too, in which many Americans had won honors both from Great Britain and France. But the attack at Cantigny was the first distinct American advance.

The Americans penetrated the German positions to the depth of nearly a mile. Their artillery completely smothered the Germans, and its whirr could be heard for many miles in the rear. Twelve French tanks supported the American infantry. The artillery preparation lasted for one hour, and then the lines of Americans went over the top. A strong unit of flame throwers and engineers aided the Americans. The American barrage moved forward a hundred yards in two minutes and then a hundred yards in four minutes. The infantry followed with clock-like precision. Fierce hand-to-hand fighting occurred in Cantigny, which contained a large tunnel and a number of caves. The Americans hurled hand grenades like baseballs into these shelters.

The attack had been carefully planned and was rehearsed by our infantry with the tanks. In every detail it was under the direction of the Superior French Command, to whom much of the credit for its success was due. The news of the American success created general satisfaction among the French and English troops. The operation, of course, was not one of the very greatest importance. It was a sort of an experiment, but coming as it did, in the middle of the great German Drive, it was ominous. America had arrived.

On May 30th General Pershing announced the complete repulse of further enemy attacks from the new American positions near Cantigny. This time he says: "there was considerable shelling with gas, but the results obtained were very small. The attempt was a complete failure. Our casualties were very light. We have consolidated our positions."

The London *Evening News* commenting on this fact says: "Bravo the young Americans! Nothing in today's battle narrative from the front is more exhilarating than the account of their fight at Cantigny. It was clean cut from beginning to end, like one of their countrymen's short stories, and the short story of Cantigny is going to expand into a full-length novel which will write the doom of the Kaiser and Kaiserism. Cantigny will one day be repeated a thousand fold."

The Germans, in reporting this fight, avoided mention of the fact that the operation had been conducted by American troops. This seemed to indicate that they feared the moral effect of such an admission in Germany. Up to this time, with the exception of small brigades, the American army had been held as a reserve. After the Cantigny fight they were hurried to the front. The main point to which they were sent at first was Château-Thierry, north of the Marne, the nearest point to Paris reached by the enemy. There, at the very critical point of the great German Drive, they not only checked the enemy but, by a dashing attack, threw him back.

This may be said to be the turning point in the whole war. It not only stopped the German Drive at this point, but it gave new courage to the Allies and took the heart out of the Germans. The troops were rushed to the battle front at Thierry, arriving on Saturday, June 1st. They entered the battle enthusiastically, almost immediately after they had arrived. A despatch from Picardy says: "On their way to the battle lines they were cheered by the crowds in the villages through which they passed; their victorious stand with their gallant French Allies, so soon after entering the line, has electrified all France."

General Pershing's terse account of what happened reads as follows: "In the fighting northwest of Château-Thierry our troops broke up an attempt of the enemy to advance to the south through Veuilly Woods, and by a counter-attack drove him back to the north

CHAPTER XLVII

REDEMPTION OF THE HOLY LAND

FROM the beginning of the war the German General Staff and the British War Office planned the occupation of Palestine and Macedonia. Germany wanted domination of that territory because through it lay the open road to Egypt and British prestige in the East. Turkey was the cat's paw of the Hun in this enterprise. German officers and German guns were supplied to the Turks, but the terrible privations necessary in a long campaign that must be spent largely in the desert, and the inevitable great loss in human life, were both demanded from Turkey.

Great Britain made no such demands upon any of its Allies. Unflinchingly England faced virtually alone the rigors, the disease and the deaths consequent upon an expedition having as its object the redemption of the Holy Land from the unspeakable Turk.

Volunteers for the expedition came by the thousands. Canada, the United States, Australia and other countries furnished whole regiments of Jewish youths eager for the campaign. The inspiration and the devotion radiating from Palestine, and particularly from Jerusalem and Bethlehem, drew Jew and Gentile, hardy adventurer and zealous churchman, into Allenby's great army.

It was a long campaign. On February 26, 1917, Kut-el-Amara was recaptured from the Turks by the British expedition under command of General Sir Stanley Maude, and on March 11th following General Maude captured Bagdad. From that time forward pressure upon the Turks was continuous. On September 29, 1917, the Turkish Mesopotamian army commanded by Ahmad Bey was routed by the British, and historic Beersheba in Palestine was occupied on October 31st. The untimely death of General Maude, the hero of Mesopotamia, on November 18, 1917, temporarily cast gloom over the Allied forces but it had no deterrent effect upon their successful operations. Siege was laid to Jerusalem and its environs late in November, and on December 8, 1917, the

Holy City which had been held by the Turks for six hundred and seventy-three years surrendered to General Allenby and his British army. Thus ended a struggle for possession of the holiest of shrines both of the Old and New Testaments, that had cost millions of lives during fruitless crusades and had been the center of religious aspirations for ages.

General Allenby's official report follows:

"I entered the city officially at noon December 11th with a few of my staff, the commanders of the French and Italian detachments, the heads of the political missions, and the military attachés of France, England, and America.

"The procession was all afoot, and at Jaffa gate I was received by the guards representing England, Scotland, Ireland, Wales, Australia, New Zealand, India, France and Italy. The population received me well.

"Guards have been placed over the holy places. My military governor is in contact with the acting custodians and the Latin and Greek representatives. The governor has detailed an officer to supervise the holy places. The Mosque of Omar and the area around it have been placed under Moslem control, and a military cordon of Mohammedan officers and soldiers has been established around the mosque. Orders have been issued that no non-Moslem is to pass within the cordon without permission of the military governor and the Moslem in charge."

JERUSALEM UNDER MARTIAL LAW

A proclamation in Arabic, Hebrew, English, French, Italian, Greek and Russian was posted in the citadel, and on all the walls, proclaiming martial law and intimating that all the holy places would be maintained and protected according to the customs and beliefs of those to whose faith they were sacred. The proclamation read:

PROCLAMATION

To the Inhabitants of Jerusalem the Blessed and the People Dwelling in its Vicinity:

The defeat inflicted upon the Turks by the troops under my command has resulted in the occupation of your city by my forces. I, therefore, here now proclaim it to be under martial law, under which form of administration it will remain so long as military consideration make necessary.

However, lest any of you be alarmed by reason of your experience at the hands of the enemy who has retired, I hereby inform you that it is my desire that every person should pursue his lawful business without fear of interruption.

Furthermore, since your city is regarded with affection by the adherents of three of the great religions of mankind, and its soil has been consecrated by the prayers and pilgrimages of multitudes of devout people of these three religions for many centuries, therefore, do I make it known to you that every sacred building, monument, holy spot, shrine, traditional site, endowment, pious bequest, or customary place of prayer of whatsoever form of the three religions will be maintained and protected according to the existing customs and beliefs of those to whose faith they are sacred.

Guardians have been established at Bethlehem and on Rachel's tomb.   The tomb at Hebron has been placed under exclusive Moslem control.

The hereditary custodians at the gates of the Holy Sepulchre have been requested to take up their accustomed duties in remembrance of the magnanimous act of the Caliph Omar, who protected that church.

Jerusalem was now made the center of the British operations against the Turks in Palestine. Mohammed V, the Sultan of Turkey, died July 3, 1918, and many superstitious Turks looked upon that event as forecasting the end of the Turkish Empire. The Turkish army in Palestine was left largely to its fate by Germany and Austria, and although it was numerically a formidable opponent for General Allenby's forces, that distinguished strategist fairly outmaneuvered the Turkish High Command in every encounter. The beginning of the end for Turkish misrule in Palestine came on September 20th when the ancient town of Nazareth was captured by the British.

A military net was thereupon closed upon the Turkish army. The fortified towns of Beisan and Afule followed the fate of Nazareth. In one day's fighting 18,000 Turkish prisoners, 120 guns, four airplanes, a number of locomotives and cars, and a great quantity of military and food supplies were bagged by the victorious British. So well did Allenby plan that the British losses were far the smallest suffered in any large operation of the entire war. It was the swiftest and most decisive victory of any scored by the Allies. It ended the grandiose dream of Germany for an invasion of Egypt in stark disaster, and swept the Holy Land clear of the Turks.

This great battle on the Biblical field of Armageddon was remarkable in that it was virtually the only engagement during

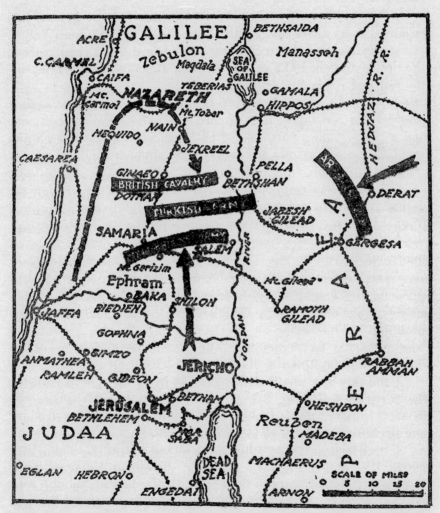

HOW THE TWO WINGS OF THE BRITISH ARMY TRAPPED THE TURKS.

the entire war offering the freest scope to cavalry operations. British cavalry commands operated over a radius of sixty miles between the Jordan and the Mediterranean, sweeping the Turks before them. The official story of the battle contained the following description:

"By 8 P. M., on September 20th, the enemy resistance had collapsed everywhere save on the Turkish left in the Jordan Valley.

"Our left wing, having swung around to the east, had reached the line of Bidieh, Baka and Messudieh Junction, and was astride the rail and roads converging at Nabulus.

"Our right wing, advancing through difficult country against considerable resistance, had reached the line of Kahn Jibeit, one and a quarter miles northeast of El-Mugheiar, and Es-Sawieh and was facing north astride the Jerusalem-Nabulus road.

"On the north, our cavalry, traversing the field of Armageddon, had occupied Nazareth, Afule and Beisan and were collecting the disorganized masses of enemy troops and transports as they arrived from the south. All avenues of escape open to the enemy, except the fords across the Jordan between Beisan and Jisr-Ed-Dameer, were thus closed.

"East of the Jordan Arab forces of the King of Hedjaz had effected numerous demolitions on the railways radiating from Deraa, several important bridges, including one in the Yurmak Valley, having been destroyed.

"Very severe losses have been inflicted on the masses of Turkish troops retreating over the difficult roads by our air services.

"A German airplane, later ascertained to have been carrying mails, landed in the midst of our troops at Afule. The pilot, who believed the place still to be in Turkish hands, destroyed the machine and its contents before he could be secured.

"By 9 o'clock on Saturday night, on our left wing, the infantry about Birafur had reached the line Beitdejan-Samaria-Birafur shepherding the Germans in the west of the Jerusalem-Nabulus road into the arms of our cavalry operating southward from Jenin and Beisan.

"Other enemy columns vainly attempted to escape into the Jordan Valley in the direction of Jisr-Ed-Dameer These columns suffered severely from our aircraft, which constantly harassed them with bombs and machine gunfire from low altitudes.

CHAPTER LI

LAST DAYS OF THE WAR

FROM November 1st until November 11th, the day when the armistice granting terms to Germany was signed, the collapse of the German defensive was complete. The army that under von Hindenburg and Ludendorf had smashed its way over Poland, Roumania, Serbia, Belgium, and into the heart of France, was now a military machine in full retreat. It is only justice to that machine to say that the great retreat at no place degenerated into a rout. Von Hindenburg and the German General Staff had planned a series of rear-guard actions that were effective in protecting the main bodies of infantry and artillery. Machine-gun nests and airplane attacks were the main reliance of the Germans in these maneuvers of delay, but the German field artillery also did its share.

Immense quantities of material and many thousands of prisoners were captured by the British, Canadians and Australians in the north, and by the French and Americans in the south. Simultaneously with this wide and savage drive upon the Germans along the Belgian and French fronts, came the heaviest Italian attack of the war. Before it the Austrians were swept in a torrent that was irresistible. French, English and American troops co-operated in this thrust that extended from the plains of the Piave into Trentino. The immediate effect of the Italian offensive was to force Austria to her knees in abject surrender. An armistice, humiliating in its terms, was signed by the Austrian representatives, and the back door to Germany was opened to the Allies.

Germany's frantic plea for an armistice followed. There were those in the Allied countries who maintained that nothing short of unconditional surrender should be permitted. Cooler counsel prevailed, and an armistice was offered to the German High Command through General Foch, the terms of which far exceeded in severity those granted to Turkey and Austria. These were read for the first time by Germany's representatives on Friday, November 8th.   General Foch, when he gave the document to the German delegation, declared that Germany's decision must be made within seventy-two hours.   Eleven o'clock on Monday, November 11th, was the time limit permitted to Germany.   The armistice was signed by General Foch and the German representatives on the morning of November 11th, but fighting did not actually cease until eleven o'clock, several hours after the terms had been agreed to.   This was in accordance with arrangement made between the signers.

THE SEDAN OF 1918

Sedan, where Marshals McMahon and Bazaine, commanding the armies of Napoleon III, surrendered to the King of Prussia in 1870, marked the last notable victory of the American forces in France.   The Sedan of 1870 marked the birth of German militarism.   The Sedan of 1918 marked its death.

Preceding the advance of the Americans upon Sedan, came a cloud of aviators in pursuit and bombing planes, headed by the famous aces of the American forces.   The first and second divisions of the First Army led the way.   In the van of the second division were the Marines, whose heroism in Bellau Wood marked the beginning of Germany's end.   The famous Rainbow Division made the most savage thrust of the action, pursuing the foe for ten miles and sweeping the Freya Hills clear of machine nests and German artillery.

The last action of the war for the Americans followed immediately on the heels of the battle of Sedan.   It was the taking of the town of Stenay.   The engagement was deliberately planned by the Americans as a sort of battle celebration of the end of the war. The order fixing eleven o'clock as the time for the conclusion of hostilities, had been sent from end to end of the American lines. Its text follows:

1. You are informed that hostilities will cease along the whole front at eleven o'clock A. M., November 11, 1918, Paris time.

2. No Allied troops will pass the line reached by them at that hour in date until further notice.

3. Division commanders will immediately sketch the location of their line.   This sketch will be returned to headquarters by the courier bearing these orders.

4. All communication with the enemy, both before and after the termination of hostilities, is absolutely forbidden. In case of violation of this order severest disciplinary measures will be immediately taken. Any officer offending will be sent to headquarters under guard.

5. Every emphasis will be laid on the fact that the arrangement is an armistice only and not a peace.

6. There must not be the slightest relaxation of vigilance. Troops must be prepared at any moment for further operations.

7. Special steps will be taken by all commanders to insure strictest discipline and that all troops be held in readiness fully prepared for any eventuality.

8. Division and brigade commanders will personally communicate these orders to all organizations.

Signal corps wires, telephones and runners were used in carrying the orders and so well did the big machine work that even patrol commanders had received the orders well in advance of the hour. Apparently the Germans also had been equally diligent in getting the orders to the front line. Notwithstanding the hard fighting they did Sunday to hold back the Americans, the Germans were able to bring the firing to an abrupt end at the scheduled hour.

The staff and field officers of the American army were disposed early in the day to approach the hour of eleven with lessened activity. The day began with less firing and doubtless the fighting would have ended according to plan, had there not been a sharp resumption on the part of German batteries. The Americans looked upon this as wantonly useless. It was then that orders were sent to the battery commanders for increased fire.

Although there was no reason for it, German ruthlessness was still rampant Sunday, stirring the American artillery in the region of Dun-sur-Meuse and Mouzay to greater activity. Six hundred aged men and women and children were in Mouzay when the Germans attacked it with gas. There was only a small detachment of American troops there and the town no longer was of strategical value. However, it was made the direct target of shells filled with phosgene. The enemy hurled them into the town until every street reeked with gas.

THE LAST TOWN TO FALL

Poorly clad and showing plainly evidences of malnutrition, the inhabitants crowded about the Americans, kissing their hands and hailing them as deliverers. They declared they had had no meat for six weeks. They virtually had been prisoners of war for four years and were overwhelmed with joy when they learned that an armistice was probable.

The last French town to fall into American hands before the armistice went into effect was Stenay. Patrols reported they had found it empty not more than a quarter of an hour before eleven o'clock. American troops rushed through the town and in a few minutes Allied flags were beginning to appear from the windows. As the church bell solemnly tolled the hour of eleven, troops from the Ninetieth Division were pouring into the town.

Two minutes before eleven o'clock the firing dwindled, the last shells shrieking over No Man's Land precisely on time.

SURRENDER OF GERMAN FLEET

On November 21st the German high seas fleet that had been protected by the submarines surrendered to the combined fleet consisting of British, American and French battleships. The British Admiralty statement upon this spectacle follows:

The commander-in-chief of the Grand Fleet has reported that at 9.30 o'clock this morning he met the first and main installment of the German high seas fleet, which is surrendering for internment.

Admiral Sir David Beatty is commander-in-chief of the Grand Fleet.

Another flotilla of German U-boats also was surrendered today to a British squadron. There were nineteen submarines in all; the twentieth which should have come today, broke down on the way.

The Grand Fleet, accompanied by five American battleships and three French cruisers, steamed out at 3 o'clock this morning from its Scottish base to accept the surrender. The vessels moved in two long columns.

The German fleet which surrendered consisted of nine battleships, five cruisers, seven light cruisers and fifty destroyers. Seventy-one vessels in all. There remain to be surrendered two battleships, which are under repair, and fifty modern torpedo-boat destroyers.

One German destroyer while on its way across the North Sea

CHAPTER LII

The Drastic Terms of Surrender

THE end of the war came with almost the dramatic suddenness of its beginning. Bulgaria, hemmed in by armies through which no relief could penetrate, asked for terms. The reply came in two words, "Unconditional Surrender."

Turkey, witnessing the rout of her army in Palestine by the great strategist, General Allenby, and a British army, asked for an armistice. The Porte signed without hesitation an agreement comprising twenty-five severe requirements.

The surrender of Bulgaria and Turkey forced Austria's hand. The terms under which it was permitted to capitulate were even harder than those granted to Turkey. They comprised eighteen requirements divided into military and naval clauses.

Germany, proud, imperial Germany, met the greatest humiliation of all the Teutonic allies when the Kaiser and the German High Command were brought to their knees. Thirty-five clauses, the most severe and drastic ever demanded from a great power, were included in the armistice agreement. Only the imminent menace of an invasion of Germany would have sufficed to compel the German representatives to sign such a document. Following are the drafts of the Turkish, Austrian and German armistice agreements.

THE TURKISH AGREEMENT

1. The opening of the Dardanelles and the Bosporus and access to the Black Sea. Allied occupation of the Dardanelles and Bosporus forts.

2. The positions of all mine fields, torpedo tubes and other obstructions in Turkish waters are to be indicated, and assistance given to sweep or remove them, as may be required.

3. All available information concerning mines in the Black Sea is to be communicated.

4. All Allied prisoners of war and Armenian interned persons and prisoners are to be collected in Constantinople and handed over unconditionally to the Allies.

5. Immediate demobilization of the Turkish army, except such troops as are required for surveillance on the frontiers and for the maintenance of internal order. The number of effectives and their disposition to be determined later by the Allies after consultation with the Turkish Government.

6. The surrender of all war vessels in Turkish waters or waters occupied by Turkey. These ships will be interned in such Turkish port or ports as may be directed, except such small vessels as are required for police and similar purposes in Turkish territorial waters.

7. The Allies to have the right to occupy any strategic points in the event of any situation arising which threatens the security of the Allies.

8. Use by Allied ships of all ports and anchorages now in Turkish occupation and denial of their use by the enemy. Similar conditions are to apply to Turkish mercantile shipping in Turkish waters for the purposes of trade and the demobilization of the army.

9. Allied occupation of the Taurus Tunnel system.

10. Immediate withdrawal of Turkish troops from Northern Persia to behind the pre-war frontier already has been ordered and will be carried out.

11. A part of Transcaucasia already has been ordered to be evacuated by Turkish troops. The remainder to be evacuated if required by the Allies, after they have studied the situation.

12. Wireless, telegraph and cable stations to be controlled by the Allies. Turkish Government messages to be excepted.

13. Prohibition against the destruction of any naval, military or commercial material.

14. Facilities are to be given for the purchase of coal, oil, fuel and naval material from Turkish sources, after the requirements of the country have been met. None of the above materials are to be exported.

15. The surrender of all Turkish offices in Tripolitania and Cyrenaica to the nearest Italian garrison. Turkey agrees to stop supplies and communication with these officers if they do not obey the order to surrender.

16. The surrender of all garrisons in Hedjaz, Assir, Yemen, Syria and Mesopotamia to the nearest Allied commander, and withdrawal of Turkish troops from Cilicia, except those necessary to maintain order, as will be determined under Clause 6.

17. The use of all ships and repair facilities at all Turkish ports and arsenals.

18. The surrender of all ports occupied in Tripolitania and Cyrenaica, including Mizurata, to the nearest Allied garrison.

19. All Germans and Austrians, naval, military or civilian, to be evacuated within one month from Turkish dominions, and those in remote districts as soon after that time as may be possible.

20. Compliance with such orders as may be conveyed for the disposal of equipment, arms and ammunition, including the transport of that portion of the Turkish army which is demobilized under Clause 5.

CHAPTER LIII

GENERAL PERSHING'S OWN STORY*

SUMMARY OF THE OPERATIONS OF THE AMERICAN ARMY FROM MAY 26, 1917, TO NOVEMBER 11, 1918

Immediately upon receiving my orders I selected a small staff and proceeded to Europe in order to become familiar with conditions at the earliest possible moment.

The warmth of our reception in England and France was only equaled by the readiness of the commanders-in-chief of the veteran armies of the Allies and their staffs to place their experience at our disposal. In consultation with them the most effective means of co-operation of effort was considered. With French and British armies at their maximum strength, and all efforts to dispossess the enemy from his firmly intrenched positions in Belgium and France failed, it was necessary to plan for an American force adequate to turn the scale in favor of the Allies. Taking account of the strength of the central powers at that time, the immensity of the problem which confronted us could hardly be overestimated. The first requisite being an organization that could give intelligent direction to effort, the formation of a General Staff occupied my early attention.

GENERAL STAFF

A well-organized General Staff through which the commander exercises his functions is essential to a successful modern army. However capable our division, our battalion, and our companies as such, success would be impossible without thoroughly coordinated endeavor. A General Staff broadly organized and trained for war had not hitherto existed in our army. Under the commander-in-chief, this staff must carry out the policy and direct the details of administration, supply, preparation, and operations of the army as a whole, with all special branches and bureaus subject to its control. As models to aid us we had the veteran French

*Taken from General Pershing's report to the Secretary of War, November 20, 1918

Our entry into the war found us with few of the auxiliaries neces-sary for its conduct in the modern sense. Among our most impor-tant deficiencies in material were artillery, aviation and tanks. In order to meet our requirements as rapidly as possible, we accepted the offer of the French Government to provide us with the neces-sary artillery equipment of seventy-fives, one fifty-five millimeter howitzers, and one fifty-five G P F guns from their own factories for thirty divisions. The wisdom of this course is fully demonstrated by the fact that, although we soon began the manufacture of these classes of guns at home, there were no guns of the calibers mentioned manufactured in America on our front at the date the armistice was signed. The only guns of these types produced at home thus far received in France are 109 seventy-five millimeter guns.

In aviation we were in the same situation, and here again the French Government came to our aid until our own aviation program should be under way. We obtained from the French the necessary planes for training our personnel, and they have provided us with a total of 2,676 pursuit, observation, and bombing planes. The first airplanes received from home arrived in May, and altogether we have received 1,379. The first American squadron completely equipped by American production, including airplanes, crossed the German lines on August 7, 1918. As to tanks, we were also com-pelled to rely upon the French. Here, however, we were less fortu-nate, for the reason that the French production could barely meet the requirements of their own armies.

It should be fully realized that the French Government has always taken a most liberal attitude and has been most anxious to give us every possible assistance in meeting our deficiencies in these as well as in other respects. Our dependence upon France for artillery, aviation and tanks was, of course, due to the fact that our industries had not been exclusively devoted to military pro-duction. All credit is due our own manufacturers for their efforts to meet our requirements, as at the time the armistice was signed we were able to look forward to the early supply of practically all our necessities from our own factories.

The welfare of the troops touches my responsibility as Com-mander-in-Chief to the mothers and fathers and kindred of the men who came to France in the impressionable period of youth. They could not have the privilege accorded European soldiers during their

CHAPTER LIV

AMERICA'S POSITION IN WAR AND PEACE

BY common consent of the Entente Allies, President Wilson was made the spokesman for the democracy of the world. As Lloyd George, Premier Clémenceau of France, Premier Orlando of Italy, and other Europeans recognized, his utterances most clearly and cogently expressed the principles for which civilization was battling against the Hun. More than that, these statesmen and the peoples they represented recognized that back of President Wilson were the high ideals of an America pledged to the redemption of a war-weary world.

The war produced a sterility in literature. Out of the great mass that was written, however, two productions stood out in their nobility of thought and in their classic directness of expression. These were the address before Congress by President Wilson on the night of April 2d, 1917, when, recognizing fully the dread responsibility of his action, he pronounced the words which led America into the World War, and the speech made by him on Monday, November 11, 1918, when addressing Congress he announced the end of the war. Other declarations of the President that will be treasured as long as democracy survives, are those enunciating the fourteen points upon which America would make peace, and two later declarations as to America's purposes.

His address of April 2d was delivered before the most distinguished assemblage ever gathered within the hall of the House of Representatives. The Supreme Court of the United States, headed by the Chief Justice, every member of the embassies then resident in Washington, the entire membership of the House and Senate, and a host of the most distinguished men and women that could crowd themselves into the great hall, listened to what was virtually America's Declaration of War.

The air was still and tragic suspense was upon every face as the President began his address. At first he was pale as the marble rostrum against which he leaned. As he read from small sheets typewritten with his own hand, his voice grew firmer and the flush of indignation and of resolution overspread his countenance.   He said:

GENTLEMEN OF THE CONGRESS:

I have called the Congress into extraordinary session because there are serious, very serious, choices of policy to be made, and made immediately, which it was neither right nor constitutionally permissible that I should assume the responsibility of making.

On the third of February last I officially laid before you the extraordinary announcement of the Imperial German Government that on and after the first day of February it was its purpose to put aside all restraints of law or of humanity and use its submarines to sink every vessel that sought to approach either the ports of Great Britain and Ireland on the western coasts of Europe or any of the ports controlled by the enemies of Germany within the Mediterranean.   That had seemed to be the object of the German submarine warfare earlier in the war, but since April of last year the Imperial Government had somewhat restrained the commanders of its undersea craft in conformity with its promise then given to us that passenger boats should not be sunk and that due warning would be given to all other vessels which its submarines might seek to destroy, when no resistance was offered or escape attempted, and care taken that their crews were given at least a fair chance to save their lives in their open boats.   The precautions taken were meager and haphazard enough, as was proved in distressing instance after instance in the progress of the cruel and unmanly business, but a certain degree of restraint was observed.   The new policy has swept every restriction aside.   Vessels of every kind, whatever their flag, their character, their cargo, their destination, their errand, have been ruthlessly sent to the bottom without warning and without thought of help or mercy for those on board, the vessels of friendly neutrals along with those of belligerents.   Even hospital ships and ships carrying relief to the sorely bereaved and stricken people of Belgium, though the latter were provided with safe conduct through the proscribed areas by the German Government itself and were distinguished by unmistakable marks of identity, have been sunk with the same reckless lack of compassion or of principle.

I was for a little while unable to believe that such things would in fact be done by any government that had hitherto subscribed to the humane practices of civilized nations.   International law had its origin in the attempt to set up some law which would be respected and observed upon the seas, where no nation had right of dominion and where lay the free highways of the world.   By painful stage after stage has that law been built up, with meager enough results, indeed, after all was accomplished that could be accomplished, but always with a clear view, at least, of what the heart and conscience of mankind demanded.   This minimum of right the German Government has swept aside under the plea of retaliation and necessity and because it had no weapons which it could use at sea except these which it is impossible to employ as it is employing them without throwing to the winds all scruples of humanity or of respect for the understandings that were supposed to underlie the intercourse of the world. I am not now thinking of the loss of property involved, immense and serious as that is, but only of the wanton and wholesale destruction of the lives of non-combatants, men, women, and children, engaged in pursuits which have always, even in the darkest periods of modern history, been deemed innocent and legitimate. Property can be paid for; the lives of peaceful and innocent people can not be. The present German submarine warfare against commerce is a warfare against mankind.

It is a war against all nations. American ships have been sunk, American lives taken, in ways which it has stirred us very deeply to learn of, but the ships and people of other neutral and friendly nations have been sunk and overwhelmed in the waters in the same way. There has been no discrimination. The challenge is to all mankind. Each nation must decide for itself how it will meet it. The choice we make for ourselves must be made with a moderation of counsel and a temperateness of judgment befitting our character and our motives as a nation. We must put excited feeling away. Our motive will not be revenge or the victorious assertion of the physical might of the nation, but only the vindication of right, of human right, of which we are only a single champion.

When I addressed the Congress on the twenty-sixth of February last I thought that it would suffice to assert our neutral rights with arms, our right to use the seas against unlawful interference, our right to keep our people safe against unlawful violence. But armed neutrality, it now appears, is impracticable. Because submarines are in effect outlaws when used as the German submarines have been used against merchant shipping, it is impossible to defend ships against their attacks as the law of nations has assumed that merchant-men would defend themselves against privateers or cruisers, visible craft giving chase upon the open sea. It is common prudence in such circumstances, grim necessity indeed, to endeavor to destroy them before they have shown their own intention. They must be dealt with upon sight, if dealt with at all. The German Government denies the right of neutrals to use arms at all within the areas of the sea which it has proscribed, even in the defense of rights which no modern publicist has ever before questioned their right to defend. The intimation is conveyed that the armed guards which we have placed on our merchant ships will be treated as beyond the pale of law and subject to be dealt with as pirates would be. Armed neutrality is ineffectual enough at best; in such circumstances and in the face of such pretensions it is worse than ineffectual: it is likely only to produce what it was meant to prevent; it is practically certain to draw us into the war without either the rights or the effectiveness of belligerents. There is one choice we can not make, we are incapable of making: we will not choose the path of submission and suffer the most sacred rights of our nation and our people to be ignored or violated. The wrongs against which we now array ourselves are no common wrongs; they cut to the very roots of human life.

Summarized Chronology of the War

1914

June

28.—Assassination of Archduke Francis Ferdinand, heir to throne of Austria-Hungary, and his wife at Sarajevo, Bosnia.

July

28.—Austria-Hungary declares war on Serbia.

29.—Russian mobilization ordered.

August

1.—Germany declares war on Russia.

1.—France orders mobilization.

2.—Germany demands free passage through Belgium.

3.—Germany declares war on France.

3.—Belgium rejects Germany's demand.

4.—Germany at war with Belgium. Troops under Gen. Von Kluck cross border. Halted at Liège.

4.—Great Britain at war with Germany. Kitchener becomes Secretary of War.

5.—President Wilson tenders good offices of United States in interests of peace.

6.—Austria-Hungary at war with Russia.

7.—French forces invade Alsace. Gen. Joffre in supreme command of French army.

7.—Montenegro at war with Austria.

7.—Great Britain's Expeditionary Force lands at Ostend, Calais and Dunkirk.

8.—British seize German Togoland.

8.—Serbia at war with Germany.

8.—Portugal announces readiness to stand by alliance with England.

11.—German cruisers *Goeben* and *Breslau* enter Dardanelles and are purchased by Turkey.

12.—Great Britain at war with Austria-Hungary.

12.—Montenegro at war with Germany.

17.—Belgian capital removed from Brussels to Antwerp.

19.—Canadian Parliament authorizes raising expeditionary force.

20.—Germans occupy Brussels.

23.—Japan at war with Germany. Begins attack on Tsingtau.

24.—Germans enter France near Lille.

25.—Austria at war with Japan.

26.—Louvain sacked and burned by Germans. Viviani becomes premier of France.

28.—British fleet sinks three German cruisers and two destroyers off Heligoland.

28.—Austria declares war on Belgium.

29.—Russians invest Konigsberg, East Prussia. New Zealanders seize German Samoa.

30.—Amiens occupied by Germans.

31.—Russian army of invasion in East Prussia defeated at Tannenberg by Germans under Von Hindenburg.

31.—St. Petersburg changed to Petrograd by imperial decree.

September

3.—Paris placed in state of siege; government transferred to Bordeaux.

3.—Lemberg, Gallicia, occupied by Russians.

4.—Germans occupy Rheims.

6-10.—Battle of Marne. Von Kluck is beaten by Gen. Joffre, and the German army retreats from Paris to the Soissons-Rheims line.

10.—*Emden*, German cruiser, carries out raids in Bay of Bengal.

14.—French reoccupy Amiens and Rheims.

19.—British forces begin operations in Southwest Africa.

20.—Rheims cathedral shelled by Germans.

24.—Allies occupy Peronne.

25.—Australians seize German New Guinea.

28.—Anglo-French forces invade German colony of Kamerun.

29.—Antwerp bombardment begins.

October

2.—British Admiralty announces intention to mine North Sea areas.

6.—Japan seizes Marshall Islands in Pacific.

9.—Antwerp surrenders to Germans. Government removed to Ostend.

13.—British occupy Ypres.

14.—Canadian Expeditionary Force of 32,000 men lands at Plymouth.

15.—Germans occupy Ostend. Belgian government removed to Havre, France.

November

1.—*Monmouth* and *Good Hope*, British cruisers, are sunk by German squadron off Chile under command of Admiral Von Spee.

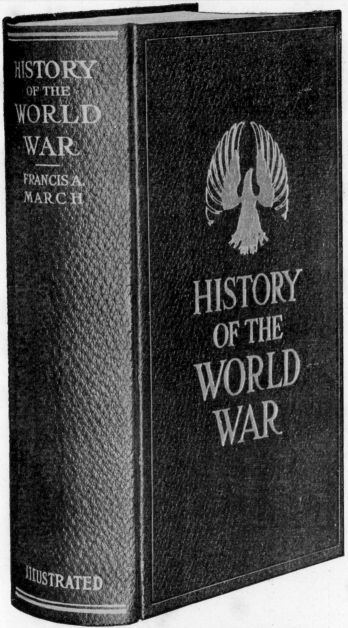

This photograph represents the LIBRARY EDITION

This entire volume is bound in FULL KRAFT LEATHER,
MOROCCO GRAINED and has colored edges. Besides its rich
appearance, it is a most durable binding, as the material is stronger
than ordinary leather. The titles of the book are stamped in gold
on both side and back.

We strongly recommend this binding which
COSTS ONLY 75 CENTS MORE than the Victory edition

NAME	ADDRESS	PRICE

NAME	ADDRESS	PRICE

NAME	ADDRESS	PRICE

NAME	ADDRESS	PRICE